INCOME TAX GUIDE for the TAXPAYER

(Assessment Year 2013-2014)

R. N. Lakhotia

VISION BOOKS

www.visionbooksindia.com

www.visionbooksindia.com

First Edition 1959
Forty-Ninth Edition 2012

ISBN - 81-7094-780-4

Published by
Vision Books Pvt. Ltd.
(Incorporating Orient Paperbacks & CARING imprints)
24 Feroze Gandhi Road, Lajpat Nagar 3
New Delhi 110024, India.
Phone: (+91-11) 2983 6470 or 2983 6480

E-mail: visionbk@vsnl.com
visionbooks@gmail.com

Printed at
Rashtra Rachna Printers
C-87 Ganesh Nagar, Pandav Nagar Complex,
Delhi-110091, India

RAM NIWAS LAKHOTIA is a well-known authority on taxation in the country. He is a regular writer and editor of several books on Income-tax, Vegetarianism, Better Living and also Humour which have gone through over 500 editions so far. He had a brilliant academic career. He stood First Class First in both the Degree and Post-Graduate Examinations in Commerce. He joined the Indian Revenue Service as I.T.O., Class-I and stood First in the whole of India in the I.T.O's Examination. He was honoured with Honorary Doctor of Taxation by Giani Zail Singh, former President of India.

As the founder President of Income Tax Payers Association and also Rajasthani Academy, National Working President of All India Vaish Federation and Life Trustee of Hindi Bhawan he is active in social service and cultural activities. He was the District Governor of Lions Clubs International in 1978-79. He is the Principal of Lakhotia College of Taxation & Management. As the Life Patron and President of Indian Vegetarian Congress of Delhi, he is spreading Vegetarianism for Health and Happiness. Mr. Lakhotia has set an ideal example of philanthropy by constructing a Big Dharmshala at Ajmer in the memory of his parents. He is the Chief Editor of monthly journal *Excellent Living*. He has delivered over 5,000 lectures on Income Tax Planning, Excellent Living and Vegetarianism which have benefited lakhs of people. Every Sunday and on other days also he answers questions on Income Tax over Zee Business T.V. channel.

Contents

PART III

Assessment of Different Assessees

PART IV

Assessment and Appellate Procedure

Preface to the 49th Edition

Several amendments have recently been made in the Income Tax Act, 1961 by the Finance Act, 2012. This 49th edition, therefore, incorporates the latest amendments made to the Income Tax Act, 1961.

A disquieting feature of the income tax legislation in India is the fact of repeated amendments effected to the IT Act. The Income Tax Act, 1961 has seen thousands of amendments since 1 April 1962 when it first came into force. The latest Finance Act, 2011 has made numerous and far-reaching changes both in the Act as well as in the tax rate structure. This makes the task of the author very difficult. Ever before he can produce a treatise containing the amendments to the act, he finds that the law has again been amended. Under the circumstances, no book on income tax law can claim to be up-to-date for long. The important changes in the Income Tax Act made by the Finance Act, 2012 have been discussed in this book at the relevant places.

This book (earlier known as *Elements of Indian Income Tax or Zero to Hero in Income Tax*) is meant for all categories of income tax payers of India. In tune with the title of this book, an attempt has been made to present the entire income tax law in a very simple manner so that even a layman, as also the students of the subject, can easily understand this complicated law.

Due to the ever-changing nature of income tax law in India all types of tax payers are facing a great deal of difficulty in their day-to-day matters relating to taxation. Without proper and up-to-date knowledge of the income tax law, it is not possible for tax payers to claim the full deductions available to them, and to compute their income correctly. Keeping this practical difficulty of tax payers in mind, I have tried to present this book for all types of income tax payers in a simple and easy-to-understand language and with the help of illustrative practical problems and their solution. I am sure this will help tax payers in the correct computation of their income and also in claiming full exemptions and deductions in their return of income.

The book could not have been completed in time without the assiduous efforts put in by my eldest son, Subhash Chandra Lakhotia, B. Com. (Hons.), I.T.P. tax guru, and personal tax planning and investment planning expert, in revising the same. Sri Kapil Malhotra deserves special thanks for the expeditious publication of this book.

May, 2012 R. N. LAKHOTIA

S-228 Greater Kailash - II
New Delhi 110048
Phone: 2921 5434
E-mail: rnlakhotia@hotmail.com
slakhotia@satyam.net.in

PART I

PRELIMINARY

CHAPTER 1

Introduction and Definitions

1. History of the Income Tax Law

Income tax is one of the most important sources of revenue in India, yet most people are not fully conversant with the law on the subject. This is because the Income tax Law in India remains a very complicated piece of legislation in spite of the several attempts made by the government from time to time at simplifying it. Rather, the complexity of this law has grown with the growth of the Act. It will be instructive as well as interesting, therefore, to present in brief the history of this important piece of legislation in India.

In this country, income tax as such was imposed for the first time in the year 1860. At that time it was quite a simple affair. After some amendments, from time to time, the law was wholly recast by the passing of the Income Tax Act of 1918. However, on the recommendations of an all-India committee appointed in 1921, the Indian Income Tax Act of 1922 was passed. The Act was materially altered several times. Thereafter the present Act, i.e., the Income Tax Act, 1961 was passed. It has repealed the old Act, i.e. the Indian Income Tax Act, 1922. The Income Tax Act, 1961 came into effect from 1 April 1962. This Act has since then seen thousands of amendments. It has also been amended by several Finance Acts, including the Finance Act, 2012.

There are at present two main Acts governing the levy of income tax in India for the Assessment Year (AY) 2012-2013 and AY 2013-2014:

The Income Tax Act, 1961: This is the main enactment; and

The Finance Act, 2012: The Finance Act is passed each year by the Parliament. It fixes the rates of tax to be charged for the assessment year in question as well as the rates of tax to be charged for advance payment of tax, etc. It has also been used for the purpose of effecting amendments in the main IT Act.

The sections referred to in this book are the sections of the Income Tax Act, 1961.

There are subsidiary rules known as the Income Tax Rules, 1962, and several notifications and CBDT (Central Board of Direct Taxes) circulars which also govern the levy of income-tax in India, Besides, there are Press releases to clarify the I.T. Law.

2. Types of Income Tax Levies

Income tax in India comprises only of the following two levies:

Income Tax

Income tax on companies is, however, popularly known as Corporation Tax in the Union Budget.

Surcharge & Cesses

Additional emergency duty is occasionally levied on income tax. It is for the purposes of the Union.

For the Assessment Year 2012-2013, as per the Finance Act, 2012 no surcharge would be payable by individuals and HUFs. For companies and firms, the rate of surcharge would be 5% for the Assessment Year 2013-14 on income in excess of ₹ 1 crore. For the A.Y. 2013-2014 there will be an additional surcharge of 2% on I.T. and S.C. known as "Education Cess" and Secondary and Higher Education Cess of 1% on I.T. and S.C.

3. Units of Assessment, i.e. Persons Liable to Income Tax — Section 2(31)

Only the following types of persons are liable to pay income tax:(1) Individual; (2) Hindu Undivided Family (HUF); (3) Company; (4) Firm; (5) Any other association of persons (AOP) or a body of individuals (BOI), whether incorporated or not; (6) Local authority; and (7) Every artificial juridical person, e.g. an idol, deity, etc.

4. Heads of Income — Section 14

The various heads of income, profits and gains chargeable to income tax are as follows:

(1)	Salaries	Sections 15 to 17
(2)	Income from house property	Sections 22 to 27

Contd . . .

(3)	Profits and gains of business or profession	Sections 28 to 44D
(4)	Capital gains	Sections 45 to 55
(5)	Income from other sources	Sections 56 to 59

5. Tax Liability

For the A.Y. 2011-2012 the exemption limit for male individuals, Hindu undivided families, association of persons, body of individuals, etc. is ₹ 1,60,000. The income slabs and the income tax rates are as under:

A. For A. Y. 2012-2013
The basic exemption limits and the rates of income-tax will continue to be the same as those specified for assessment year 2010-2011. However, the tax slabs are as under:

Upto	₹1,80,000 of total income	Nil
From	₹1,80,001 to ₹5,00,000	10 %
From	₹5,00,001 to 8,00,000	20 %
Above	₹8,00,000	30 %

In the case of every individual, being a woman resident in India, and below the age of sixty years at any time during the previous year:

Upto	₹1,90,000	Nil
From	₹1,90,001 to ₹5,00,000	10 %
From	₹5,00,001 to 8,00,000	20 %
Above	₹8,00,000	30 %

In the case of every individual, being a resident in India, who is of the age of sixty years or more at any time during the previous year:

Upto	₹2,50,000	Nil
From	₹2,50,001 to ₹5,00,000	10 %
From	₹5,00,001 to 8,00,000	20 %
Above	₹8,00,000	30 %

The rates of income-tax in the case of every resident individual aged 80 years or more are as under:

Upto	₹5,00,000 of total income	Nil

From	₹5,00,001 to ₹8,00,000	20 %
Above	₹8,00,000	30 %

The Education Cess of 2% on I.T. and the "Secondary & Higher Education Cess" of 1% on I.T. would be leviable in all cases.

A company, a firm or a local authority is liable to income tax at a flat rate on its entire income, howsoever small that sum may be. For the A.Y. 2010-2011, A. Y. 2011-12 and the A.Y. 2012-13 the tax rate is 30%.

B. For A. Y. 2013-2014

The rates of income tax in the case of every individual or Hindu Undivided Family or every association of persons would be as under

Upto	₹2,00,000 of the total income	Nil
From	₹2,00,001 to ₹5,00,000	10 %
From	₹5,00,001 to ₹10,00,000	20 %
Above	₹10,00,000	30 %

The rates of income tax in the case of a resident individual aged 60 years or more but less than 80 years are as under:

Upto	₹2,50,000 of the total income	Nil
From	₹2,50,001 to ₹5,00,000	10 %
From	₹5,00,001 to ₹10,00,000	20 %
Above	₹10,00,000	30 %

The rates of income tax in the case of every resident individual aged 80 years or more are as under:

Upto	₹5,00,000 of total income	Nil
From	₹5,00,001 to 10,00,000	20 %
Above	₹10,00,000	30 %

The Education cess of 2% and the "Secondary & Higher Education Cess" of 1% on I.T. would be leviable in all cases.

The rules for the charge of income tax, corporation tax, surcharge and various allowances, etc. and the rates of tax for the A. Y. 2012-13 are explained in Chapter 23

6. Assessment — Section 2(8)

The process of determination of income or loss or refund or tax liability on an assessee is known as assessment. Generally speaking, an assessing officer makes an assessment of the income or loss of an assessee for a particular year, known as the assessment year. Besides, if any refund is due to an assessee, the computation of such refund also comes under the process of assessment. The two stages of an assessment under the Income Tax Act, 1961 are as under:

(a) Computation of total income; and
(b) Determination of income tax payable or refundable.

The definition of the expression "assessment" as given in Section 2(8) is not exhaustive. It is merely defined as follows:

"assessment" includes reassessment.

This definition merely states that the original assessment of the assessee as well as the reassessment of the assessee in a case when the same is reopened under the Income Tax Act, are also included under the expression "assessment".

7. Assessment Year (or AY) — Section 2(9)

The assessment of an assessee under the Income Tax Act, 1961 is made in terms of a particular period which is known as the assessment year. Section 2(9) defines the expression "assessment year" as under:

> "Assessment year" means the period of twelve months commencing on the 1st day of April every year.

Thus, assessment year means the period of twelve months commencing from 1 April and ending on the subsequent 31 March. It is not the income earned during this period which is subject to assessment. It is only the basis of assessment in relation to a particular year which gives special significance to the expression "assessment year". Under the Income Tax Act, 1961 income tax is charged for each assessment year on the total income of an assessee of a period which is known as previous year. The expression "previous year" is defined in para 8 below.

8. Previous Year — Section 3

It is the income of assessee in the previous year which is liable to tax. The term "previous year" is spoken of in relation to the term "assessment year" and is a period of 12 months, or less, in the immediately preceding financial year. The tax is levied on the income of the previous year at the rate or rates given in the Finance Act passed by the Parliament each year.

Thus, income is made in one year known as the previous year and income tax thereon is levied in the following year known as the assessment year.

For example, the previous year for the A.Y. 2012-2013 is the financial year 2011-2012, i.e. from 1.4.2011 to 31.3.2012 and the previous year for the A.Y. 2013-2014 is the financial year 2012-2013, i.e. from 1.4.2012 to 31.3.2013.

9. Assessee — Section 2(7)

"Assessee" means a person by whom income tax or any other sum of money is payable under this Act. In addition, it includes:

(a) Every person in respect of whom any proceeding under the Income Tax Act, 1961 has been taken for the assessment of his income or any other person in respect of which he is assessable, or of the loss sustained by him or by such other person, or of the amount of refund due to him or to such other person.

(b) Every person who is deemed to be an assessee under any provision of the Act, e.g. a representative assessee.

(c) Every person who is deemed to be assessee in default under any provision of the Act, e.g. an assessee who does not pay the instalment of advance tax in time is deemed to be an assessee in default by Section 218.

10. Income — Section 2(24)

Income tax as the term itself signifies, is a tax on income. But curiously enough the Act does not adequately define the term "income". Its meaning is more or less similar to the layman's understanding of its being equal to money or money's worth periodically received from a definite source. It may be taken to denote anything which comes in and that too, from some outside source. Broadly speaking, it does not include capital receipts or windfall gains or casual income. However, it would be worthwhile knowing various items which are included in the term "income" by virtue of Section 2(24) of the Act. Thus "income" is made to include

- profits and gains,
- dividend, and also
- certain allowances and benefits.

Capital receipts like gift and amounts received on inheritance are not treated as income.

Certain gifts to be taxable as income — Sections 2(24) (xiii), 10(39) and 56(2)(v)

Any gift received on or after 1.10.2009 by an individual or an H.U.F. from any person, in cash or by way of credit in excess of ₹50,000 would be liable to tax as "Income from other sources". In the case of an individual's marriage, such additional gifts without any upper limit would be exempt. Gifts received or credited by an individual from a relative out of natural love would be exempted. So also gifts received or credited by any individual or an H.U.F. under a will or by way of inheritance or in contemplation of death of the payer or donor or from any local authority or from any fund or foundation or university or other educational institution or hospital or other medical institution or any trust or institution referred to in Section 10(23C) or registered under Section 12AA will not be taxable as income. For the individual, "relative" would mean his spouse, brother or sister, spouse's brother or sister, parent's brother or sister, lineal ascendant or descendant of self or spouse. Spouse of these persons would also be considered as relative.

Thus, the sum of money received from local authority, or any fund or foundation or university or hospital or other medical institution as mentioned in Section 10(23C) or the trust or institution registered under Section 12AA would be exempted without any upper limit. However, gifts in kind are also taxable as income, if the aggregate value of all gifts is in excess of ₹50,000 per year. However, gifts received on the occasion of marriage are fully exempt.

This means that if any gift is received, say from a Charity Trust by a meritorious student for higher studies, say of ₹4 lakh, then such amount would be exempted from being taxed as income as per Section 56. Similarly, if any help is received from some Trust, etc. for medical treatment, say of ₹3 lakh then also it would be tax exempt. However, this benefit would not be available on grant for education or medical help if received from an institution from abroad because the same is not covered in the exemption clause as the exemption is only for Trusts or Institutions mentioned in Section 10(23C) or Section 12 AA of the Income-tax Act, 1961.

From 1-10-2009 the immovable property received without consideration, the shares & securities, jewellery, drawings, paintings, etc., if received from non-relatives would be added as taxable income.

From 1-6-2010 "Bullion" received from non-relatives would be taxable as income.

11. Agricultural Income — Section 2 (1A)

All types of income are not taxable. There are certain incomes which are non-taxable. Agricultural income is one of them. Therefore, its definition is very important.

Thus agricultural income means:

(A) Any rent or revenue provided it fulfils the following conditions:

(i) that it is derived from land;
(ii) that the land is situated in India; and
(iii) that the land is used for agricultural purposes:

(B) Any income derived from such land by

(i) agriculture, i.e. by actual cultivation of land and by means of certain basic operations in agriculture; or
(ii) by the performance of some agricultural process ordinarily employed by the cultivator, etc. to render the produce fit to be taken to market; or
(iii) by the sale of the produce, in respect of which no other process (other than ii above) has been employed.

(C) Any income derived from any building owned and occupied by the receiver of the rent or revenue of any such land, or occupied by the cultivator or the receiver of rent-in-kind, of any land with respect to which any process mentioned in (ii) and (iii) of sub-clause (B) is carried on, subject to certain conditions about the building being on or in the vicinity of the land, etc.

The Finance Act, 2000 inserted a new Explanation in Section 2(1A) to clarify that any income from such building or land arising from the use of the building or land for any purpose other than agriculture, would not be included in the definition of "agricultural income". For example, if a person has income from using such building or land for purposes, such as letting it out for residential purposes or for the purposes of any business or profession, then such income would not be treated as agricultural income from the A.Y. 2001-2002.

Any income derived from saplings and seedlings grow in a nursery would be agricultural income and thus be fully exempt from tax on and from the A.Y. 2009-10. Under Rule 8, where the assessee himself grows tea leaves and manufactures tea in India 40% of the profits on sales is taxable as business income and 60% is exempt as agricultural income.

12. Total Income — Section 2(45)

Different types of assessees have to pay tax on different types of income, according to the basis of their residence, as described in

Chapter IV. Thus, the term "total income" means the total amount of income referred to in Section 5 computed in the manner laid down in the Act.

The term "Gross total income" as per Section 80B (5) means the total income computed without making any deduction under Chapter VIA, e.g. for 5-year Bank F.Ds, L.I.P., etc. as per Section 80C.

13. Exempted Income

In arriving at the taxable liability of an assessee, the words "exempted income" simply mean that income which is included in the total income but which is otherwise exempt from income tax. A rebate is allowed on such income at an average rate calculated with reference to his total income.

14. Permanent Account Number (or PAN) — Section 139 A

The assessees have been required to make an application in Form No. 49A in duplicate for allotment of a Permanent Account Number in compliance with the provisions of Section 139A. Vide Notification No. S.O. 889(E) dated 9.10.1998 rule 114B has been inserted for compulsory quoting of PAN for specified transactions. Thus, it is provided in rule 114B that every person would be required to quote his Permanent Account Number or General Index Register Number in all documents pertaining to the specified transactions. The application for allotment of PAN can be made to the income-tax department or to their authorised agents. Presently the Unit Trust of India is authorised to accept applications for PAN.

15. Authorised Representative — Section 288

Excepting when an assessee is required to be personally present before any income tax authority or Appellate Tribunal he has a right to be represented by an "Authorised representative" who is any person authorised by him in writing to appear on his behalf, being

(i) a relative or a person regularly employed by him; or

(ii) any officer of a scheduled bank with which the assessee maintains a current account or has other regular dealings; or

(iii) any legal practitioner who is entitled to practise in any civil court in India; or

(iv) any chartered accountant, or any auditor within the meaning of Section 226 of the Companies Act 1956; or certain other persons under Section 288.

CHAPTER 2

Income Tax Authorities, The Appellate Tribunal and Settlement Commission

1. Income Tax Authorities — Sections 116 to 138

For the discharge of executive and appellate functions relating to the administration of the Income Tax Act, the various classes of income tax authorities are re-constituted w.e.f. 1 October 1998. The provisions relating to the appointment, control, jurisdiction, powers and functions are described below.

2. The Central Board of Direct Taxes

This is the highest executive authority constituted by the Central Board of Revenue Act, 1963 which came into force wef 1 January 1964. It consists of a few members, one of whom is the chairman. It has the power to make rules for the purpose of this Act. This is also known as the "Board" or CBDT.

3. Directors-General or Directors or Joint Directors of Income Tax

The Government of India may appoint as many directors-general or directors or joint directors of income tax as it thinks fit. They shall perform such functions of any other income tax authority as may be assigned to them by the Board. They are generally in charge of research, vigilance, inspection, investigation, exemption, etc.

4. Chief Commissioners, Commissioners and Joint Commissioners of Income Tax

The central government may appoint as many chief commissioners, commissioners and joint commissioners of income tax as it thinks fit. They perform their functions in respect of such areas, or of such persons or classes of persons, or such income or such cases as the Board may direct.

5. Commissioner of Income Tax (Appeals)

The first appeal to Commissioner of Income Tax (Appeals) [CIT (Appeals)] broadly lies in cases where the order is made by the Assessing Officer from 1 October 1998.

6. Deputy Commissioners of Income Tax

The central government may appoint as many Deputy Commi-ssioners of Income tax [DCs] as it thinks fit. The function of DC(A) is to make assessment on the assessees. The other DC supervises the work of ITOs, etc.

7. Assistant Commissioners of Income Tax

They (ACs) are also appointed by the Central Government. They are directly under the control of the commissioners or coint commissioners and perform such functions regarding assessment, survey, etc., as may be assigned to them by the former.

8. Income Tax Officers

An Income Tax Officer is the most important official of the department. He is generally the actual Assessing Officer (AO) who initiates assessment, calls for a return from assessees within his jurisdiction, makes the assessment , collects revenue and makes the refunds. He, along with the AC or the specially empowered DC is known as assessing officer as per Section 2(7A) since all of them now do the same assessment work.

9. Inspectors of Income Tax

They are appointed by the commissioners of income tax and perform such functions in the execution of the IT Act as are assigned to them by any other income tax authority under whom they are appointed to work.

10. Provisions Relating to Searches and Seizures — Sections 132, 132A and 132B

The main provisions relating to searches and seizures are as under:

(a) Director general or director or the chief commissioner or commissioner or any such deputy director or deputy commissioner, as may be empowered by the Board, have been authorised to issue search warrants.

(b) The power of search has been extended to persons, vehicles, vessels and aircrafts also, in addition to premises.

(c) The CCIT and the CIT have each been empowered to authorise search and seizure irrespective of whether the person with respect to whom the search is authorised is assessed in his jurisdiction or not, if the building, etc. to be searched is within his jurisdiction and he considers that any delay would be prejudicial to the interest of the revenue.

(d) If in the course of search certain assets, account books and documents are found at the premises of an assessee, there is a rebuttable presumption that such assets, books of account, etc. belong to the assessee, that their contents are true and that the signature and hand-writing are of the persons who can reasonably be assumed to have signed or written the books of account, etc.

As per the Finance Act, 2003 far reaching amendments were made to the procedure relating to search and seizure cases. These amendments came into force from 1.6.2003:

(i) The system of Block assessment in search cases was dispensed with. In the alternative new procedure has been framed as contained in new Sections 153A, 153B and 153C of the Income Tax Act, 1961.

(ii) Under the new procedure for completion of assessment in search cases the Assessing Officer shall issue notice to such person requiring him to furnish, within such period as may be prescribed in the notice, return of income in respect of six assessment years immediately preceding the assessment year relevant to the previous year in which the search was conducted under Section 132 or requisition under Section 132A.

(iii) After receiving the Income-tax Returns, the Assessing Officer shall assess or reassess the total income of each of the six assessment years.

(iv) The provisions of penal interest, penalty as well as prosecution would apply to the assessee in respect of all those assessments which are completed in search cases. In respect of assessments or reassessments made in respect of an assessment under the above section, the tax shall be chargeable at the rate or rates as are applicable to such assessment year.

(v) The Assessing Officer shall make an order of assessment or reassessment in respect of each assessment year, falling within six assessment years under Section 153A within a period of two years from the end of the financial year in which the last of the authorisations for search under Section 132 or requisition under Section 132A were executed.

(vi) If the Assessing Officer is satisfied that any money, bullion, jewellery or other valuable article or thing or books of account or documents seized or requisitioned belong or belongs to a person other than the assessee then the seized books of account, or documents or assets seized or requisitioned shall be handed over to the Assessing Officer having jurisdiction over such other person and the tax authorities shall proceed against such other person.

(vii) The appeal against the order of assessment or reassessment under Section 153A shall lie with the Commissioner of Income Tax (Appeals).

(viii) No surrender shall be taken from the assessees by the search team.

(ix) Stock-in-trade shall not be seized or restrained during the course of search.

(x) The seized assets shall be released if the concerned person makes an application to the Assessing Officer within 30 days from the end of the month in which the asset was seized.

As per the Finance Act, 2005 a time limit for making assessment or reassessment of the total income would be either two years or the end of the financial year in which the warrant of authorization, etc. was executed or one year from the end of the financial year in which books of account or documents or assets seized or requisitioned are handed over to the Assessing Officer having jurisdiction over such other person, whichever is later. These have been made retrospectively from 1 June 2003.

11. Survey by IT Authority — Sections 133A and 133 B

The following are the salient features of survey by the IT authorities under Section 133A:

(a) The powers are available to the Income Tax Authority being the

CIT, the DI, the DD, the DC, the AD and the AO and in some cases the Inspector also.

(b) The I.T. Authority may check cash, stock or valuables found in the business premises.

(c) The Income Tax Authority may record statement of any person in the business premises.

(d) The Income Tax Authority may require furnishing of information which may be useful for, or relevant to any proceeding under the Act.

(e) The assessee would be required to afford facility to enable the authority to visit any other premises, besides the business premises where the assessee states that any part of his books of account, cash, stock, etc. are kept.

The income tax authorities have also been empowered to collect information and record statement of the persons concerned at any time after an event, function, or ceremony, but well before the stage of assessment proceedings in the following year where they are of the opinion that having regard to the nature, scale or extent of the expenditure incurred it is necessary to do so under Section 133A.

12. Income Tax Appellate Tribunal (ITAT) — Sections 252 to 255

It is appointed by the Central Government and consists of as many persons as the Government thinks fit. It consists of two types of members:

(a) Judicial members, and

(b) Accountant members.

13. Disclosure of Information — Sections 138 & 280

A person may be making an application to the Commissioner in Form No. 46 to get any information relating to any assessee in respect of any assessment made provided the Commissioner is satisfied that it is in the public interest so to do.

14. Income Tax Settlement Commission — Sections 245A to 245L

No application for settlement can be made unless the additional income tax on the disclosed income exceeds ₹10,00,000.

An order of settlement generally provides for the terms of settlement including any demand by way of tax, penalty or interest, the manner of payment of the sum due under the settlement, etc. The commission may, if it is satisfied that the applicant has cooperated with it in the proceedings before it and has made full and true disclosure of his income and the manner in which it has been derived, grant to the applicant full or partial immunity from prosecution and penalty.

The salient changes in the settlement scheme are:

(a) The Settlement Commission would pass an order within nine months from the end of the month in which the application was received.

(b) The Settlement Commission would not grant immunity form the prosecution under any law other than Income Tax Act and Wealth Tax Act.

(c) The Commission would not have powers to reopen the complete proceedings where the application under Section 245C has been filed on or after 1.6.2007.

(d) On or after 1.6.2007, an assessee can apply for settlement only once during his life time.

(e) The minimum tax involved was increased from ₹1 lakh to ₹10 lakh,

(f) Now the matters concerning Income-tax Raid can also be settled by the Income-tax Settlement Commission in case the minimum tax involved is ₹50 lakh.

CHAPTER 3

Basis of Charge

I. Residential Status of Assessees

1. Classification of Persons Liable to Tax on the Basis of Residence — Section 6

The tax liability of a person is determined by reference to his residence in India in the previous year. For this purpose the assessees are divided into the three classes, namely:

- Resident but not ordinarily resident;
- Resident and ordinarily resident; and
- Non-resident.

2. Individuals

(A) Resident But Not Ordinarily Resident — Section 6(1)

An individual is a resident in India in any previous year if he fulfils any one of the following two conditions:

(a) That he is in India in that year for 182 days or more, or
(b) That he has been in India for atleast 365 days in the four years immediately preceding that year, and is in India for 182 days or more in that year, on a visit to India.

It is further provided that where an individual who is a citizen of India leaves India in any year for the purposes of employment outside India or is a citizen who leaves India as member of the crew of an Indian ship, he will not be treated as resident in India in that year unless he has been in India in that year for 182 days or more. The effect of this amendment will be that the "test" of residence will stand modified to that extent in such cases.

A person is said to be "not ordinarily resident" in India in any previous year if such person is:

(a) An individual who has been a non-resident in India in nine out of the ten previous years preceding that year, or has during the seven previous years preceding that year been in India for a period of, or periods amounting in all to, seven hundred and twenty-nine days or less; or

(b) A Hindu undivided family whose manager has been a non-resident in India in nine out of the ten previous years preceding that year, or has during the seven previous years preceding that year been in India for a period of, or periods amounting in all to, seven hundred and twenty-nine days or less.

(B) Resident and Ordinarily Resident or "Ordinary Resident" — Section 6(6)

An individual becomes an ordinary resident in India if he does not qualify for "Not ordinarily resident" in India as per para (A) above.

> **N.B.:** The period of 182 days, etc. referred to above need not be continuous or at the same place.

(C) Non-Resident

An individual is non-resident in India in any year if he does not fulfil any of the two conditions laid down in first part of para 2(A).

3. Other Assessees

(1) A Hindu Undivided Family (HUF) is resident in India if any portion of the control and management of its affairs is situated in the country. An HUF is ordinarily resident if its Karta is resident and ordinary resident in India.

(2) A firm or other association of persons is resident in India if any portion of the control and management of its affairs is situated here.

(3) A company is resident in India if any one of the following two conditions is fulfilled:

   (a) The control and management of its affairs is situated wholly in India, or

   (b) It is an Indian company.

   A company is ordinarily resident if it is resident in India.

(4) Every other person is resident in India unless the control and management of his affairs is situated wholly outside India.

II. Scope of Total Income — Section 5

The classification of various assessees on the basis of their residence in India is not an end in itself. The purpose is quite obvious. The taxation liability of various types of assessees varies with their residence. The table given below will show the difference in the incidence of taxation on different assessees on the basis of residence.

TABLE 1

Scope of total Income or Incidence of Taxation — Section 5

(A) Resident and Ordinarily Resident	(B) Resident but Not Ordinarily Resident	(C) Non-resident
Such persons are charged on		
Indian Income:		
1. All income re ceived or deemed to be received in India in the previous year by or on behalf of such person.	1. The same as in para 1 of column (A)	1. The same as in para 1 of column (A)
2. Income accruing or arising or deemed to accrue or arise to him in India in the previous year.	2. The same as in para 2 of column (A)	2. The same as in para 2 of column (A).
Note: From A.Y. 2004-05 please refer to new definition of Section 6 (6)		
Foreign Income:		
3. Income accruing or arising outside India in the previous year (not received in India) in India.	3. Income accruing or arising outside India and derived from a business or profession set up in India	3. Nil
(*Note*. There is no tax on foreign remittances of past profits or income in any case).		

On a careful perusal of the above table we find that a non-resident has to pay tax only on his Indian income while a resident has to pay tax on his Indian as well as foreign income subject, of course, to certain conditions described above.

4. Income Deemed to be Received — Section 7

The following incomes are deemed to be received in the previous year:

(i) The annual accretion in the previous year to the balance at the credit of an employee participating in a recognised provident fund as consists of:

  (a) contributions made by the employer in excess of 10% of the salary of the employee; and

  (b) interest credited on the balance to the credit of theemployee in so for as it exceeds a rate higher than the rate fixed by the Central Government, such rate being 8% per annum. (However, inquiry should always be made about the latest rate).

(ii) The transferred balance in a recognised provident fund in accordance with the rules.

5. Income Deemed to Accrue or Arise in India — Section 9

The following income shall be deemed to accrue or arise in India:

(i) All incomes accruing or arising, whether directly or indirectly, through or from any business connection in India, or through or from any property in India, or through or from any asset or source of income in India, or through the transfer of a capital asset, situated in India. Certain exceptions have been laid down to this clause;

(ii) income which falls under the head "Salaries", if it earned in India;

(iii) income chargeable under the head "Salaries", payable by the government to a citizen of India for service outside India;

(iv) a dividend paid by an Indian company outside India;

(v) Income by way of interest payable by the Government, and in some other special cases of NRIs, etc;

(vi) income by way of royalty payable by the Government or a resident or a non-resident in some cases;

(vii) income by way of fees or technical services payable by the government or a resident or a non-resident in some cases.

PROBLEM NO. 1.

Mr. Shyam Kumar was in India for 32 days during the year ending on 31.3.2012. His income in India is ₹1,42,000 and in USA it is $48,000. Compute his income tax liability in India for the A.Y. 2012-13.

SOLUTION

No Income-tax would be payable by Shyam Kumar on his income outside India as he is a Non-Resident Indian. He will pay Income-tax in India on his Indian income only, which would be nil because his taxable Indian income is below ₹ 1,80,000, i.e. the taxable limit.

CHAPTER 4

Exemptions, Rebates and Reliefs

Introduction

The Income Tax Act, tax payers complain, is a very harsh Act. But this statement is only half true, for the Act allows several kinds of exemptions, allowances, deductions, rebates and reliefs to the assessees.

This chapter deals with different types of exemptions, rebates and reliefs scattered all over the Income Tax Act. For the sake of convenience the chapter is divided into three parts: I. Exemptions; II. Rebates; III. Reliefs.

Incomes which are totally or partially exempt from tax are described under "Exemptions", while incomes which are subject to tax but which are entitled to rebate or relief at an average rate of tax in certain circumstances are discussed under "Rebates" or "Reliefs." Besides, there are certain deductions granted in computing total income, which are described in Chapter XII.

I. Exemptions

The Income Tax Act has given a list of several types of incomes which are either fully exempt from tax or partially exempt from tax. They have been divided into the following types:

(A) **Fully exempted income,** i.e., incomes which are exempt from income tax and are not to be included in the total income at all.

(B) **Partially exempted income,** i.e. incomes which are included in the total income for rate purposes but are themselves exempt either wholly or partially from income tax.

(C) **Special provision for newly established industrial undertaking in Free Trade Zones and 100% EOUs, etc.**

Fully Exempted Incomes — Sections 10 to 13

Income of religious and charitable trusts and institutions — Sections 11 to 13 & 80 G.

The income of charitable trusts and institutions would be so exempt from income tax if the specified modes of investment are used. Likewise, the

Charitable Trusts and Educational Institutions are also allowed to accumulate the income to the extent of 15% of the income of the year which will be treated as the amount spent for charities. The Charity Trust can also accumulate its income for five years. In certain cases the income of the educational institutions is fully exempt from Income-tax. As per the Finance Act, 2006 the anonymous donations received by a charity trust (with certain exceptions) would be taxed @ 30%.

As per the Taxation Laws (Amendment) Act, 2005 certain procedural changes were made. Such trusts and institutions have to file their income tax return in case the gross amount exceeds the maximum exempt amount and also to get the audit done.

Where an application for registration of a new charitable or religious trust or institution is made on or after 1.6.2007, the provisions of exemption under Section 11 and 12 would apply in relation to the assessment year immediately following the financial year in which such application is made. Thus, a trust, etc. would no longer be required to file an application for registration within one year from the date of its creation or establishment. Besides, the power of the CIT to grant registration for past years by condonation of delay has been removed. This amendment was made by the Finance Act, 2007 and was effective from 1.6.2007.

The "advancement of any object of general public utility" would not be a charitable purpose if it involves the carrying on any activity in the nature of trade, commerce or business or any service in relation thereto for a fee or cess or any other consideration, irrespective of the nature of use or application of income from such activity or the retention of such income, by the concerned entity. This amendment is as per the Finance Act, 2008 from the A.Y. 2009-2010. However, the Finance Act, 2010 has clarified that gross receipts upto ₹10 lakh would not violate the law even if it involves carrying on an activity in the nature of trade.

Other Fully Exempted Income — Section 10

The following main types of income are completely exempt from tax (income tax and surcharge) and are not to be included in the total income of any assessee for any previous year:

(1) Agricultural Income [Section 10(1)] — as described in chapter I, para 11.

(2) Receipts from HUF [Section 10(2)] — i.e. any sum received by an individual as a member of a Hindu undivided family where such sum has been paid out of the income of the family or, in the case of any impartible estate belonging to the family.

(3) Share from a firm [Section 10 (2A)]. In the case of a person being a partner of a firm which is assessed as such his share in the total income of the firm.

(4) Casual income [Section 10 (3)] — Not exempt w.e.f. A.Y. 2003-2004.

(5) Certain income of a non-resident [Section 10 (4)]. In the case of a non-resident, any income from interest on, or from premium on the redemption of any bonds issued by the Central Government as may be notified in the Official Gazette, and any interest on money standing to the credit of a Non-resident (External) account in any bank in India in accordance with the Foreign Exchange Regulation Act, 1973 and any rules made thereunder for a person resident outside India as per FERA.

(6) Exemption of interest income of non-residents from specified savings certificates [Section 10 (4B)]. In the case of non-resident Indian citizens and foreign nationals of Indian origin income by way of interest on specified savings certificates, e.g. NSC (IV & VII Series) subscribed in foreign currency in accordance with the Foreign Exchange Management Act, 1999 and any rules made thereunder.

(7) Value of travel concession [Section 10(5)]. LTA is exempted for journey on leave to any part of India. The exemption in respect of LTA (Leave Travel Assistance) in available in respect of the employee himself and his family including the spouse and two children from 1-10-1998. If the children are born prior to 1-10-1998, there is no restriction with regard to the number. The parents and brothers and sisters are also included if they are wholly or mainly dependent on him. The amount of LTA exemption is limited to the amount of expenses actually incurred.

Rule 2B(2) of the IT Rules, 1962 provides that the LTA exemption available to an employee is limited to two journeys only which are performed in a block of 4 calendar years. The initial calendar year commences from the calendar year 1986 where the journey is performed on or after 1-4-89. Thus, in the first block there are 4 calendar years, i.e. 1986, 1987, 1988 & 1989. The present block is of the years 2010, 2011, 2012 and 2013. The employee will be eligible to any two journeys to be performed in 4 calendar years, which alone will be entitled to LTA exemption. It is provided in Rule 2B(3) that where such LTA is not availed of by the employee during any block of four calendar years, an amount in respect of the value of the travel concession or assistance, if any, first availed of by the individual during first calendar year of the immediately succeeding year shall be eligible for exemption.

(8) Certain incomes of non-citizen of India [Section 10 (6). The following are some of the important types of incomes exempted in the case of an individual who is not a citizen of India:

(i) Passage money or the value of any free or concessional passage received by or due to such individual from his employer for himself, his spouse and children in connection with his proceeding on home leave out of India or after retirement or termination of service or for his children having full time education outside India in connection with their proceeding to India during vacation.

(ii) The remuneration received by him as an official of an embassy, etc. of a foreign State for service in such capacity as a member of staff.

(iii) The remuneration received by him as an employee of a foreign enterprise for services rendered by him during his stay in India, provided certain conditions are fulfilled:

(iv) The remuneration received by employees of foreign states during their stay in India in connection with their training in any establishment or office of the Government or any public sector under taking will be exempt.

(9) Death-cum-retirement gratuity [Section 10(10)]. Any death-cum-retirement gratuity received by all categories of employees of the Central Government or State Government or the local authority or of a corporation established by a Central, State or Provincial Act or any payment of retiring gratuity received under the Pension Code is fully exempt. For private sector employees any gratuity not exceeding half a month's salary for each year of completed service, calculated on the basis of the average salary for the ten months immediately preceding the year in which the gratuity is paid, subject to a maximum of ₹10 lakh.

(10) Commuted value of pensions [Section 10(10A)]. The following types of commuted pensions will be so exempt:

(i) Any payment in commutation of pension received by all categories of Central Government and State Government employees or employees of a local authority or a corporation established by a Central, State or Provincial Act.

(ii) Any payment in commutation of pension received under any scheme of any other employer, to the following extent only: (a) In a case where the employee receives any gratuity, the commuted value of one-third of the pension which he is normally entitled to receive; and (b) In any other case, the commuted value of 50% of such pension.

(iii) Any payment in commutation of pension received from a fund of the LIC under section 10(23 AAB), as per amendment by the Finance (No. 2) Act, 1996, from the AY 1997-98.

(11) Exemption of amount received by way of encashment of unutilised earned leave by retiring employees [Section 10 (10AA)]. Leave encashment salary from income tax in the case of retiring employees of the Central Government or a State Government. In the case of other employees, the exemption is to be determined with reference to the leave to his credit at the time of retirement, (whether on superannuation or otherwise) subject to a maximum of ten months' leave. The exemption will be limited to the amount payable for such unutilised leave on the basis of the 'average salary' of the employee or the notified sum, whichever is less. For this purpose, the entitlement to leave shall not exceed 30 days for every year of service and "average salary" shall be determined on the basis of the salary drawn for the ten immediately preceding months. In relation to non-Government employees the Central Government is empowered, by notification in the Official Gazette to raise the aforesaid monetary ceiling, keeping in view the maximum amount which will qualify for exemption in the case of Government servants. It is ₹3,00,000.

(12) Exemption of retrenchment compensation paid to workers [Section 10(10B)]. Retrenchment compensation received by a workman under the Industrial Disputes Act, 1947 or under any other Act or under any Rule or modification issued under any laws, as also retrenchment compensation received by workman under any award or contract of service or otherwise. The exemption will, however, be limited to the amount calculated in accordance with the provisions of Section 25F(b) of the Industrial Disputes Act, 1947, or the notified amount viz., ₹5 lakhs (vide Notification No.10969 dated 25.6.1999) whichever is less.

(13) Amount received by employees of public sector or other companies on voluntary retirement or separation upto ₹5 lakh, subject to rules as per Section 10(10C) in respect of a VRS.

(14) Tax on Perquisite of Employees. As per the Finance Act, 2002 w.e.f. A.Y. 2003-2004 [as per Section 10(10CC)] the tax on perquisite actually paid by the employer on behalf of the employee would not be treated as income of the employee.

(15) Amount received under insurance policy and bonus other than under a Key Man Insurance Policy as per Section 10 (10D) and also as per the Finance Act, 2003 on any sum received under an insurance policy issued on or after 1-4-2003 in respect of which the premium payable for any of the years during the term of the policy exceeds 20% of the actual capital sum assured. This would not apply in the event of death of the policy holder.

(16) Any payment from a statutory provident fund [Section 10(11)]. Any payment from a P.F. to which the Provident Funds Act, 1925 applies or any other P.F. set up by the Central Government and notified in the Official Gazette e.g., PPF.

(17) The accumulated balance of an R.P.F. [Section 10(12)]. Such sum due and becoming payable to an employee participating in recognised provident fund to the extent provided in the Rule 8 of part A of the IV Schedule.

(18) Any payment from a superannuation fund [Section 10(13)]. Made on the death of a beneficiary or in lieu of or in commutation of an annuity or by way of refund of contribution on the death of a beneficiary or on his leaving the service, etc.

(19) House rent allowance [Section 10(13A)]. Any special allowance specially granted to an assessee by his employer to meet expenditure actually incurred on payment of rent (by whatever name called) in respect of residential accommodation occupied by the assessee to such extent as prescribed by Rule 2A.

(20) Any special allowance or benefit [Section10(14)]. Any special allowance or benefit not being in the nature of a perquisite under Section 17(2) specially granted to meet expenses wholly, necessarily and exclusively incurred in the performance of the duties of an office or employment of profit, to the extent to which such expenses are actually incurred for that purpose, as may be notified in the Official Gazette.

As per Rule 2BB conveyance allowance and travelling allowance specifically granted to an employee to meet expenses wholly, necessarily and exclusively in the performance of the duties of an office or employment of profit is exempt from income tax.

As per the above rule any allowance or any type of allowance to meet the ordinary daily charges incurred by an employee on account of absence from his normal place of duty is also exempt from income tax, provided such allowance is actually incurred to meet the ordinary daily charges of the employee.

Vide Rule 2BB certain cost of living allowances are exempt. Such allowances are Composite Hill Compensatory Allowance, Special Compensatory Allowance, Tribal Areas Allowance, Allowance of Transport Workers, Children Educational Allowance and Hostel

Allowance. Also Helper allowance, Academic pursuits allowance and Uniform allowance are fully exempt.

(21) Certain types of interest payment, etc. [Section 10(15).

(i) Income by way of interest, premium or redemption or any other payment on such securities, bonds, annuity certificates, savings certificates & other certificates issued by the Central Government and deposits as the Central Government may, by notification in the Official Gazette, specify in this behalf, subject to such conditions as may be specified in the said notification.

(ii) In the case of individuals and HUFs interest on Relief Bonds and 6.5% Savings Bonds, 2003.

(iii) Interest on Gold Deposit Bonds.

(iv) Post office savings bank interest.

(v) Interest on specified bond of a local authority or a state-pooled finance entity.

(22) Scholarships [Section 10(16)]. The scholarships granted to meet the cost of education.

(23) Any daily allowance [Section 10(17)]. Received by any person by reason of his membership of Parliament or of any State Legislature or of any Committee thereof, any allowance received by an M.P. under the M.P. Constituency Allowance Rules, 1986 and all other allowances as may be notified. As per the Finance Act, 2006 the Constituency Allowance received by MLAs is exempt from tax.

(24) Exemption of awards and rewards [Section 10(17A)]. Any payment made, whether in cash or in kind: in pursuance of any payment instituted in the public interest by the Central Government or any State Government or instituted by any other body and approved by the Central Government in this behalf like "Lakhotia Puraskar" for best Rajasthani author, of ₹1,00,000 every year; or as a reward by the Central Government or any State Government for such purposes as may be approved by the Central Government in this behalf in the public interest.

(25) Income of certain funds [Section 10(23C)]. Any income received by any person on behalf of Prime Minister's National Relief Fund and such other similar organisations so specified.

(28) Income of mutual funds (Section 10 (23D)]. Any income of a notified mutual fund set up by a public sector bank or a public financial institution.

(27) Income of a minor upto ₹1,500, where it is clubbable in the income of a parent under Section 64(1A) as per Section 10(32).

(28) Dividends on shares of a company referred to in Section 115-O as per Section 10(34) from AY 2004-05. Income on units of UTI & Mutual Funds received from them as per Section 10(35).

(29) Income arising from transfer of long-term capital gains on shares [Section 10 (36)]. The Finance Act, 2003 has provided that any long-term capital gain regarding eligible equity shares in a company and purchased on or after 1-3-2003 but before 1-3-2004 would be exempt from tax. Eligible equity share means:

(i) any equity share in a company being a constituent of BSE-500 Index of the Stock Exchange, Mumbai as on 1-3-2003 and such transaction of purchase and sale are entered into on a recognised stock exchange in India; and

(ii) any equity share in a company allotted through a public issue on or after 1-3-2003 and listed in a recognised stock exchange in India before 1-3-2004 and such transaction is entered into on a recognised stock exchange in India.

(30) Exemption of family pension received by the family of armed forces [Section 10 (19)]. Where the death of a member of the armed forces (including paramilitary forces) of the Union has occurred in the course of operational duties, subject to prescribed conditions, the family pension received by the widow or children or nominated heirs would be exempt from tax. This amendment is operative for the A.Y. 2005-06, as per the Finance (No. 2) Act, 2004.

(31) Exemption of capital gains on compensation or compulsory acquisition of urban agricultural land [Section 10 (37)]. The capital gains arising to an individual or an HUF from agricultural land by way of compulsory acquisition or the enhanced compensation or consideration received on or after 1.4.2004 would be exempt from tax provided the land has been used for agricultural purposes during the preceding 2 years by such individual or his parent or the HUF. This amendment is operative for the A.Y. 2005-06.

(32) Exemption of long-term capital gains on securities and units [Section 10 (38)]. As per the Finance (No. 2) Act, 2004 a new tax known as "Securities transaction tax" (STT) on the value of all the transactions of purchase and sale of securities on delivery basis that take place in a recognised stock exchange in India will be levied from 1st October 2004. All long-term capital gains from such transactions would be exempt from income-tax. Tax on short-term capital gains on such securities would be charged @ 15% from the A.Y. 2009-10.

Other Exemptions

There are certain other important miscellaneous exemptions as given below:

(a) Salary & Pension of U.N. Personnel.
(b) Incomes of Political Parties, subject to some conditions.
(c) Newly established Industrial Undertakings in Free Tax Zones, etc. as per Section 10A and in SEZs as per Section 10AA.
(d) Newly established 100% EOUs as per Section 10B
(e) The tax exemption for 100% EOUs under Secion 10B and the Software Technology Park of India (STPI) under the fourth proviso of Section 10A(1) has been extended by the Finance (No. 2) Act, 2009 by one year, i.e. for the AY 2011-2012 also. Thus, the sunset clause will now be applicable from the AY 2012-2013.
(f) Ten-year tax holiday for industries set up in North–Eastern States as per Section 10C.
(g) Income of the North-Eastern Development Finance Corporation Ltd. Under Section 10(23BBF) with taxation of 20%, 40%, 60%, 80% its total income in A.Y. 2006-07, 2007-08, 2008-09 and 2009-10 respectively.
(h) Any amount received or receivable from the Central or State Government or local authority by an individual or his legal heir by way of compensation in case of disaster — Section 10 (10BC).
(i) Income by way of certain investments in venture capital undertaking in dairy or poultry industry or bio-technology, nano technology, etc. and in infrastructure facilities (as per Section 80 IB(4)
(j) Income of a Sikkimese [Section 10 (26 AAA)] from the A.Y. 1990-91, as per the Finance Act, 2008.
(k) Coir Board as per Section 10(29A)(h).
(l) Loan in the case of a reverse mortgage as per Section 10(43) on and from A.Y. 2008-09.
(m) Income of a notified Infrastructure Debt Fund [as per Section 10 (47) inserted by the Finance Act, 2011].

II. Partly Exempted Income or Income Entitled to Rebate

Income Forming Part of the Total Income but Exempt from or Entitled to Rebate of Income Tax at Average Rate — Section 86

Where the assessee is a member of an AOP, etc. assessed as per Section 67A, rebate of IT would be allowed to the member concerned.

Income Tax Rebate on Investments under Section 88

Upto the A.Y. 2005-06 a taxpayer was entitled to a rebate on the amount invested or deposited in life insurance policies, provident funds, etc. from the income tax payable by him on his total income.

The Finance Act, 2005 w.e.f. the A.Y. 2006-2007 and thereafter has omitted Section 88, hence no rebate would be permissible. However, straight deduction under Section 80C would be available @ 100% upto ₹1,00,000.

III. Reliefs

Chapter VII of the IT Act deals with the various kinds of reliefs of income tax calculated at an average rate of income tax, or in any other manner, as the case may be. Important provisions scattered throughout the Act have been described below at one place only for the sake of convenience.

Relief when Salary, etc. is Paid in Arrears or in Advance — Section 89

Appropriate relief as prescribed by Rule 21A has to be given by the AO If an assessee makes an application to the effect that his income is assessed at a rate higher than the rate at which he would have been assessed by reason of any portion of the salary being paid in arrears or by reason of receiving more than 12 months' pay in any one financial year or by reason of receiving payment which is profit in lieu of salary under Section 17(3). In the case of Government, a public sector undertaking, a company, co-operative society, local authority, university, institution, association or body such relief can be provided at the time of deduction of tax at source from the salary of the employee con-cerned, under

Section 192(2A) if Form No. 10E is given by the employee. Similarly, relief is also admissible when an assessee receives interest on securities in arrears as per Rule 21B.

Double Taxation Relief — Section 90 & 91

Double Taxation Relief would be available if the Central Government enters into an agreement with the government of any country for the purpose of providing relief on doubly assessed income in India and in that country or for the purposes of avoiding double taxation of income and may make necessary rules for the purpose.

PROBLEM No. 2

State whether the following amounts received by an assessee for the Assessment Year 2012-2013 would be liable to Income Tax:

(1) Dividend received from an agricultural company ₹95,000.

(2) Marriage gift ₹2,50,000 from a friend.

(3) Travel Assistance from employer for self and members of his family to go to Shimla, ₹18,000.

(4) Gratuity received under Payment of Gratuity Act, ₹2,90,000.

(5) Daily allowance of an employee of ₹1,000 per day and conveyance allowance of ₹5,000 p.m. (fully spent).

SOLUTION

(1) No. It would be exempt from tax under Section 10(34).

(2) It is not taxable, as it is not income under Section 56 (2) (v) proviso.

(3) It is exempt from tax under Section 10(5).

(4) It is exempt from income tax under Section 10(10)(ii).

(5) It is exempt under Section 10(14)

PART II

COMPUTATION OF INCOME

CHAPTER 5

Salaries

[SECTIONS 15 TO 17 OF I.T. ACT]

1. Introduction

Having studied the preliminary information regarding the various units of assessment, heads of income, exemptions, etc. we are now in a position to study in detail the computation of total income under the various heads. First of all we start with "Salaries".

The salient points regarding assessment of salaries are given below:

(a) The tax is payable by an assessee under the head "Salaries" in respect of any salary or wages, any annuities, pension or gratuity and any fees, commissions, perquisites or profits in lieu of, or in addition to any salary or wages, etc.

(b) Tax is levied on salaries which are due whether paid or not as well as on salaries which are paid whether due or not, e.g. advance of salary, etc., and on arrears of salary paid or allowed to him.

(c) The relationship of employer and employee must exist between the payer and the recipient of salaries. The employer may be government, a local authority, a company or any other public body or association or any other private employer.

(d) Only lumpsum received in commutation or substitution of salary or pension rights is exempt in the manner described in Chapter 4. Many persons are under the wrong impression that normal pension is exempt from tax. But pension is a part of 'Salary' as per the definition given in Section 17(1).

(e) Death-cum-retirement gratuities and certain payment from provident fund are completely exempt from tax as stated in Chapter 4.

(f) The income chargeable under the head 'Salaries' is to be computed after making certain deductions therefrom which are given below.
(g) Tax is deducted at source on salary income on a monthly basis.

2. Sums Taxable as "Salaries" — Sections 15 and 17

Under Section 15 of the IT Act, 1961 the following income is made chargeable to tax under the head salaries:
(a) any salary due from an employer or a former employer to an assessee in the previous year, whether paid or not;
(b) any salary paid or allowed to him in the previous year by or on behalf of an employer or a former employer though not due or before it became due to him; and
(c) any arrears of salary paid or allowed to him in the previous year by or on behalf of an employer or a former employer if not charged to income tax for any earlier previous year.

Thus, salary has been made taxable on "due" basis as well as on receipt basis whether due or not, e.g. advance of salary (but not a loan).

The expression "salary" has not been exhaustively defined under this Act. However, an inclusive definition of "salary" has been given in Section 17(1) whereby it is made to include:

(i) wages;

(ii) any annuity or pension;

(iii) any gratuity;

(iv) any fees, commissions, perquisites or profits in lieu of or in addition to any salary or wages;

(v) any advance of salary;

(va) any payment received by an employee in respect of any period of leave not availed of him;

(vi) the annual accretion to the balance at the credit of an employee participating in recognised provident fund to that extent to which it is chargeable to tax under Rule 6 of Part A of the IV Schedule;

(vii) the aggregate of all sums that are comprised in the transferred balance as referred to in sub-rule (2) of Rule 11 of Part A of the IV Schedule of an employee participating in a recognised provident fund, to the extent to which it is chargeable to tax under sub-rule (4) thereof.

(viii)the contribution made by the Central Government in the previous year, to the account of an employee under a pension scheme referred to in Section 80CCD.

3. Perquisites — Section 17(1) (iv) and (2)

Perquisites may be in cash as well as in kind. According to the inclusive definition given in Section 17(2), perquisite includes the following:

(i) the value of rent-free accommodation provided to assessee by his employer;

(ii) the value of any concession in the matter of rent respecting any accommodation provided to the assessee by his employer;

(iii)the value of any benefit or amenity granted or provided free of cost or at concessional rate in any of the following cases:

- (a) by a company to an employee who is a director thereof;
- (b) by a company to an employee being a person who has a substantial interest in the company;
- (c) by any employer (including a company) to an employee to whom the provisions of paragraphs (a) and (b) of this sub-clause do not apply and whose income under the head "salaries" (whether due from, or paid or allowed by, one or more employers), exclusive of the value of all benefits or amenities not provided for by way of monetary payment exceeds ₹50,000;

(iv) any sum paid by employer in respect of any obligation which, but for such payment, would have been payable by the assessee; and

(v) any sum payable by the employer, whether directly or through a fund other than a recognised provident fund or an approved superannuation fund to effect an assurance on the life of the assessee of to effect a contract for an annuity.

(vi) the value of any other fringe benefit or amenity as per I.T. Rules.

As stated above, the definition of the term perquisite as given in the Act is not an exhaustive one. The method of valuing various perquisites is described in detail in Rule 3, the provisions of which are explained below under different heads.

4. Rent-Free or Concessional Residential Accommodation — Section 17 (2) (i) and Rule 3 (1)

In the definition of the term perquisite as given in Section 17(2), we have seen that the value of rent-free accommodation or the value of any concession in the matter of rent respecting any accommodation provided by the employer to the employee is a taxable perquisite irrespective of the fact whether the salary is more or less than ₹50,000 for the year. For free-passage of employees of Railways and Air Lines, the rule is operative from 1.4.2002.

The Finance Act, 2007 has granted big relief to the employees who have been provided rent-free residential accommodation (owned by the employer or taken on lease or rent by employer). An amendment has been made in Section 17 retrospectively from the Assessment Year 2006-07 onwards whereby the rent-free residential accommodation (owned by the employer) would be valued as a perquisite @7.5% of the salary in case the accommodation is provided in cities having population upto 10 lakhs as per 2001 census. Likewise, for all those employees who have been provided such accommodation in cities having population in excess of 10 lakhs but less than 25 lakhs, the value of the perquisite would be @ 10% of salary. Finally, in case the accommodation is provided to the employees in cities with a population exceeding 25 lakhs, the perquisite value would be 15% of salary. As per the Finance Act, 2007 in respect of rent-free residential accommodation which is taken on lease or on rent by the employers, the value of perquisite would be the actual amount of lease rental paid or payable by employer or 15% of the salary, whichever is lower from this amount, the amount recovered would be deducted.

In case the accommodation is provided by the employer to the employee at a concessional rate then the perquisite value in the first case would be valued as per the above system of calculation and from the amount so arrived at, the amount recovered or received from the employee would be deducted and the balance amount would be the net value of perquisite.

Thus, big saving would be available from the tax payment by employee in respect of rent-free residential accommodation so enjoyed by him in view of amendments by the Finance Act, 2007. Same way even the employees receiving residential accommodation at a concessional amount would benefit a lot. Even the Income-tax (13th Amendment) Rules 2009 prescribe the above system of perquisite valuation.

PROBLEM NO. 3

A Manager of a Public Limited Company in New Delhi is in receipt of salary of ₹25,000 per month. The employee is provided with a company leased accommodation the rent for which paid by the company is ₹18,000 p.m. Furniture of the value of ₹2 lakhs has also been provided at his residence. Determine the value of perquisite for the financial year 2012-2013 relevant to A.Y. 2013-2014.

SOLUTION

The valuation of perquisite for the A.Y. 2013-2014 in terms of Rule 3 would be as under:

		Rs.
1. Perquisite value as per rule 3 (1) @ 15% of salary of ₹25,000 per month i.e. yearly	=	45,000
2. Perquisite value of in respect of furniture @ 10% of original cost of furniture	=	20,000
Total Value of Perquisite		65,000

Where the accommodation is provided by Union or State Government, then the perquisite value will be the value of license fee.

For Accommodation in Hotel (excluding for 15 days on transfer) the perquisite value would be 24% of salary.

In case two accommodation are provided then they would be taxed if it exceeds more than 90 days for transfer.

In case the accommodation is furnished then 10% of the cost of furniture, etc. would be added as a perquisite.

5. Exemption of House Rent Allowance — Section 10 (13A)

Rule 2A of the Income Tax Rules, 1962 read with Section 10(13A) provides that the maximum amount to be exempted under the head "house rent allowance" would be the lowest of the following sums:

(a) The actual amount of house rent allowance;

(b) The excess of the actual house rent over 10% of the salary.

(c) An amount equal to:

(i) where such accommodation is situated at Mumbai, Kolkata, Delhi and Chennai:

50% of the amount of salary due to the assessee in respect of the relevant period; and

(ii) where such residential accommodation is situated at any other place:

40% of the amount of salary due to the assessee in respect of the relevant period.

PROBLEM NO. 4

Mr. Z is working at Ajmer; he is getting ₹9,000 per month as salary. He is provided with a conveyance by the employer. He is getting house rent allowance of ₹8,000 per month. The actual rent paid by him is ₹9,200 per month. What is the amount of exempted H.R.A. for the F.Y. 2012-2013 relevant to the A.Y. 2013-2014?

SOLUTION

The amount of house rent allowance of Mr. Z to be excluded from taxable income would be as under:

The least or the minimum of the following three sums p.m. viz.

(a) ₹8,000, i.e. the actual amount of house rent allowance.

(b) ₹8,300, i.e. the excess of actual house rent of ₹9,200 over 10% of salary (i.e., ₹ 900 per month).

(c) ₹3,600, i.e. 40% of the salary (as the place is Ajmer).

Thus, in this case the maximum exempted house rent allowance for Mr. Z would be ₹3,600 per month i.e., the least of the above sums as per the said Rule 2A.

The term salary for the purpose includes dearness pay but excludes all other allowances and perquisites. It is the same sum which is taken for the purpose of calculating the provident fund contribution by the employee, if any.

6. Free Motor Car or Other Conveyance — Section 17(2) (iii)

From the A.Y. 2008-09, rule 3(2) has been re-introduced to provide for the valuation of this perquisite because now employer is not required to pay any FBT. Thus, broadly speaking, a sum of ₹1,800 p.m. or

₹2,400 p.m. would be added as the value of such perquisite depending on the fact whether the C.C. of the engine is upto 1.6 litres or more. Further, if a chauffeur is provided with the motor car, an additional sum of ₹900 p.m. would be added as the value of the perquisite.

7. Conveyance Allowance, Helper and Uniform, etc.

One of the most important allowances generally granted to an employee is the conveyance allowance or travelling allowance. Under the provisions of Section 10(14)(i), this allowance is completely exempt from tax, provided the same is really incurred for the purpose. If it is not incurred and there is a saving made by the employee, then the amount of saving is considered as taxable. Rule 2BB exempts:

(a) Any allowance (by whatever name called) granted to meet the cost of travel on tour or transfer. It is clarified that any sum paid in connection with transfer, packing and transportation of personal effects on such transfer is also included in the expression 'allowance granted to meet the cost of travel on transfer'.

(b) Any allowance whether granted on tour or for the purpose of journey in connection with transfer to meet the ordinary daily charges incurred by an employee on account of business from his normal place of duty.

As per Rule 2BB, Helper allowance and Uniform allowance received by an employee are also fully exempted from income tax to the extent actually spent.

The Academic Pursuits Allowance received by an employee for education in an educational institution is fully exempt.

8. Exemption of Medical Facilities — Section 17(2) (v), Proviso

Employees will be entitled to tax exemption in respect of: (i) medical facility provided in hospitals, clinics, etc. maintained by the employer; (ii) reimbursement by the employer, of expenditure incurred by the employee in hospitals, dispensaries, etc. maintained by government, local authority, or in a hospital approved under the Central Health

Scheme or a similar scheme of any state government or in a hospital approved by the Chief CIT where a certificate regarding the disease and amount of payment is furnished by the employee; (iii) group medical insurance obtained by the employer for his employees (including members of their families) or reimbursement of insurance premium to the employees who take such medical insurance; (iv) reimbursement by employer of amount spent by the employee in obtaining medical treatment from any doctor not exceeding in the aggregate ₹15,000 in a year.

As regards medical treatment abroad, the amendment seeks to exempt from tax the actual expenditure incurred on medical treatment, including the expenditure on travel and stay abroad of the patient and of one attendant in cases where an attendant is permitted by the Reserve Bank to accompany the patient. Further, this exemption would be applicable only in the case of employees whose gross total income, as computed under the Income Tax Act without including the amount reimbursed for expenditure in connection with medical treatment abroad, does not exceed ₹2,00,000.

9. Valuation of other perquisites

The valuation of other perquisites would be as under:

1.	Sweeper, Gardener, Watchman & Personal Attendant.	=	Actual cost to employer
2.	Benefit to the employee resulting from supply of gas, electric energy or water for household consumption	=	Amount paid on that account by employer less amount recovered.
3.	Free or concessional educational facilities in own institution, etc.	=	Over and above ₹1,000 per child taxed.
4.	Other free education	=	Actual cost incurred

5.	Personal or private journey free of cost or at concessional rate	= Actual cost to employer.
6.	Interest-free or concessional loan	= At the rate charged by the State Bank of India as on the first day of the previous year (less recoveries)
7.	Value of travelling, touring, accommodation for employee and any member of household.	= At the cost incurred by the employer.
8.	Free meals during office hours or at work place or through vouchers at eating joints.	= Exempt upto ₹50 per meal provided by employer.
9.	Gift vouchers	= No perquisite value on gifts below ₹5,000 if received from employer.
10.	Expenses for credit card	= Actual expenses to be taxed as perquisite value if not for office use but no perquisite if for office use.
11.	Expenditure incurred in club	= As above
12.	Use by employee of any moveable asset (other than laptop and computer).	= 10% per annum less recovery made.
13.	Transfer of moveable assets	= After deducting wear & tear @ 10% for each completed year & 50% for computers & electronic items, 20% for cars.

10. Profits in Lieu of Salary — Section 17(3)

In the definition of the word salary under Section 17(3) it has been made clear that profits in lieu of salary are included therein. The expression "profits in lieu of salary" is defined by Section 17(3) to include the following: (i) The amount of any compensation due to or received by an employee from his employer or former employer due to or received by an employee from his employer or former employer or from a provident or other fund not being an approved superannuation fund to the extent to which it does not consist of contribution by the employee or interest on such contributions.

"Profits" in relation to salary would also include amounts received in lumpsum or otherwise, prior to employment or after cessation of employment for the purposes of taxation. Fringe benefits equal to the cost to the employee would be taxable.

11. Deductions from Salary — Section 16

Three deductions are permitted to be made therefrom under Section 16. It is after allowing these deductions, as described below (and none else) that we arrive at the taxable figure of income under the head salaries.

(i) Standard Deduction

As per the Finance Act, 2005 w.e.f. the A.Y. 2006-2007 no standard deduction would be allowable from salary income.

(ii) Entertainment Allowance — Section 16 (ii)

In the case of a government servant a sum equal to 1/5th of his salary exclusive of any allowance, benefit or other perquisite or ₹5,000, whichever is less, is allowed as a deduction.

(iii) Employment Tax — Section 16 (iii)

Any sum paid as tax on employment is allowed deduction from the AY 1990-91.

PROBLEM No. 5

Mr. Rajiv Maheshwari, a renowned structural engineer has furnished particulars of his income for the year ended 31 March, 2012 and other relevant information for computing his total income as under:

(1) That he received a salary of ₹90,000 p.m. or ₹10,80,000 p.a., and a fixed entertainment allowance of ₹7,200 during the year ended 31 March 2012 from M/s. Satyapriya Engineers Ltd., Mumbai with whom he was employed as an engineer with effect from 1st April, 1995. He incurred an expenditure of ₹6,000 during the year on entertainment. He paid ₹200 as employment tax.

(2) Prior to joining M/s. Satyapriya Engineers Ltd., Bombay, he was employed by M/s. Pioneer Builders Ltd. According to his contract of service with them he was to continue for 3 years from 1st October 2006 on a salary of ₹8,000 p.m. But due to some disagreement with the management, his services were terminated with effect from 31st March, 2008 before the expiry of his term of service and he was paid ₹1,22,000 on 4th April, 2009 as compensation for loss of employment.

(3) He owned a house at Ajmer, the annual value of which was ₹43,600. It was kept reserved for his occupation. During the whole of the previous year ended 31st March, 2012 the property remained vacant as he had to remain at Mumbai, where he occupied another building throughout the year during the employment there.

Compute the total income of Mr. Rajiv Maheshwari for the assessment year 2012-2013 giving reasons for any action.

SOLUTION

Computation of total income of Mr. Rajiv Maheshwari for the assessment year 2012-2013:

	₹
1. Salaries:	
(i) Salary received from M/s. Satyapriya Engineers Ltd., Bombay @ ₹90,000 p.m.	10,80,000
(ii) Perquisite: Entertainment Allowance received during the year. [It is not deductible.	7,200
(iii) Profits in lieu of salary, being the compensation for loss of employment received from the former employer M/s. Pioneer Builders Ltd., during the previous year. [The assessee is, however, entitled to relief under Section 89].	1,22,000
Gross Salaries	12,09,200
Less: (i) Employment tax	200
	12,09,000

Contd . . .

	Rs.
2. Income from house property:	
The income in respect of the house at Ajmer and reserved for his occupation is exempt under Section 23(3)	Nil
Total Income	12,09,000

12. Contributions to Recognised Provident Funds

An employee can contribute money to the Recognised Provident Fund. On such contribution he is entitled to tax rebate U/s 88 of the Income-Tax Act, 1961. Contributions made by the employer in excess of 12% of salary is treated as deemed income. Similarly, interest credited to the PF account in excess of 8.5% p.a. as per notification under rule 6(b) of part A of 4th schedule to the I.T. Act is treated as the deemed income of an employee. For the purpose of Provident Fund "salary" would include dearness allowance only if the terms of employment so provide but excludes all other allowances.

13. Deduction for LIP and Contributions to PF, etc. — Section 80C

Refer to Chapter 11 for details.

14. Deduction in Respect of Rent Paid by an Employee Not in Receipt of House Rent Allowance — Section 80 GG

Where an employee is neither provided with a rent-free residential accommodation nor with a concessional residential accommodation nor is in receipt of house rent allowance, then he is allowed a deduction from his gross total income in respect of expenditure incurred by him on the house rent payable by him. This deduction or relief or concession is available to an employee like any other assessee under the provisions of Section 80 GG. This Section provides that in computing the total income of an assessee who is not in receipt of a house rent allowance falling within the provisions of Section 10 (13A) a deduction would be made in respect of any towards payment of house rent in respect of any furnished or unfurnished residential accommodation occupied by him. The maximum amount of such excess expenditure which is entitled to deduction is limited to ₹2,000 p.m. or 25% of his total income for the year, whichever is less.

PROBLEM No. 6

Shri Anurag is serving as Assistant Manager in a Textile Mill in Ahmedabad since 1998. Determine his Taxable Income for A.Y. 2012-2013 from the following details:

		₹	
(1)	Salary	13,000	p.m.
(2)	Dearness allowance	1,000	p.m.
(3)	Commission on Sales from employer	14,000	
(4)	Company has provided furnished residential accommodation. The Company pays rent @ ₹10,000 p.m. Value of furniture provided is ₹20,000		
(5)	Anurag's contribution to Recognised Provident Fund is @ 10% of Salary.		
(6)	Employer's Contribution to Recognised Provident Fund	18,000	p.a.
(7)	Interest credited to Recognised Provident Fund @ 8%	36,000	
(8)	Entertainment Allowance	10,000	p.a.
(9)	Interest on Bank Deposits	12,000	
(10)	Life Insurance Premium paid on own Life ₹6,000 and on the Life of Mrs. Anurag ₹5,000.		

SOLUTION

Determination of the Taxable Income of Shri Anurag for the Assessment Year 2012-2013:

	₹	₹
I. Salaries:		
(a) Salary @₹13,000	1,56,000	

Contd . . .

	₹	₹
(b) Commission on sales from employer	14,000	
(c) Entertainment Allowance "Salary" for calculating the value of Rent-Free residential accommodation as per Explanation 1 to Rule 3(a) of IT Rules, 1962.	10,000	1,80,000
(d) Dearness Allowance @ ₹1,000 p.m.		12,000
(e) Value of Rent-free Residential Accommodation : 15% "salary"		27,000
(f) Contribution of employer to Recognised Provident Fund excess of 10% of salary (₹18,000 - ₹15,600)		2,400
(g) Interest on R.P.F. (as it does not exceed the prescribed rate)		Nil
Taxable Salaries		2,21,400
II. Income from other sources:		
Interest on Deposits		12,000
Gross Total Income		2,33,400
Less: Deduction under Section 80-C		26,600
Total Income		2,06,800

The main condition for this deduction is that the assessee should file a declaration in Form No.10BA to the effect certifying that he has paid the rent to the landlord and that no other residential accommodation is owned by him or his spouse or minor children or family where he/they ordinarily resides / reside or performs/perform duties of business or employment or carries / carry on business or profession, or is owned by him or by his HUF at any other place, being accommodation in his occupation, the value of which is determined for self-occupied house property under Section 23(2)(a)(i) or 23(2)(b).

15. Option given to an Employer to pay Tax on Perquisites on behalf of the Employees — Section 192

An option to the employer to pay tax on the whole or part value of perquisite (not provided for by way of monetary payments), on behalf of any employee, without making any deduction from the income of the employee. The employer shall continue to have the option to deduct the tax on whole part of such income. Various sections also have been proposed to give consequential effect to this provision by granting credit to the employee in respect of tax so paid by the employer on behalf of the employee. Further, such tax so paid would not be treated as taxable income in the hands of the employee by virtue of Section 10(10CC).

16. Bulk filing of Returns on Computer Readable Media by certain Salaried Tax-payers

In order to enable the salaried tax-payers to fulfil their tax obligations and receive refunds, if any, within a very short period without interface with the Income Tax Department, a return could be furnished by an employee through his employer in accordance with a scheme to be notified by the Central Board of Direct Taxes for bulk filing of returns on computer readable media. In such cases, such returns would be deemed to be a return furnished under Section 139 by the employee.

17. Exemption of filing Income-tax Return to Certain Employees

As per Notification No. 51 (E) dated 12.1.2004 effective from 1-4-2004 the salaried employees having gross salary income upto ₹1,50,000 p.a. have been exempted from filing income-tax returns. However, such employees should not have any income from business or profession, capital gains and agricultural income. They should also not be in receipt of any other income from which tax has been deducted at source by any one other than the employer. To such persons the salary certificate would be issued in Form No. 16 AA vide Notification No. 50 (E) dated 12-1-2004. This Form 16AA is to be signed by the employee. It will be treated as an income-tax return the employer will submit it to I.T. department. Obtain acknowledgement and pass it over to the employee. Also note that new Income Tax Return Forms have been introduced by the Income Tax Department on and from the A.Y. 2007-2008.

CHAPTER 6

Income from House Property

[SECTIONS 22 TO 27 OF I.T. ACT]

1. Basis of Chargeability under This Head — Section 22

Under the head "Income from house property" an assessee is chargeable to tax on the annual value of certain house property:

(a) which consists of any buildings or lands appurtenant thereto,
(b) of which the assessee is the owner, and
(c) which is not occupied by the assessee for the purposes of any business carried on by him, the profits of which are chargeable to income tax.

The tax under this head is in respect of ownership and not merely the possession of the house property by an assessee. Hence income from sub-letting is charged under the head "Income from other sources".

Occupation of House Property for Business Purposes

If any part of the house property is used by the assessee for purposes of his business, no tax is charged in respect of the annual value of the part of such property. Similarly, no rent in respect of such property is allowed as a deduction from business profits.

2. Annual Value — Section 23

It is the annual value which is the subject of charge under this head.

Section 23 provides that the annual value of any property would be deemed to be:—

(a) the sum for which the property might reasonably be expected to let from year to year, or
(b) where the property or any part of the property is let and the actual rent received or receivable by the owner in respect thereof is in excess of the sum referred to in clause (a), the amount so received or receivable; or

(c) where the property or any part of the property is let, and was vacant during the whole or any part of the previous year and owing to such vacancy, the actual rent received or receivable by the owner in respect thereof is less than the sum referred to in clause (a), the amount so received or receivable.

It is further provided that the taxes levied by any local authority in respect of the properties would be deducted (irrespective of the previous year which the liability to pay such taxes was incurred by the owner according to the method of accounting regularly employed by him) in determining the annual value of the property of that previous year in which such taxes are actually paid by him. For self-occupied houses the annual value of the property shall continue to be nil. Where a house-owner owns more than one house used by him for self-occupation, then at his option he would be eligible to select one house whose annual value will be taken to be nil. The other house would, of course, be taxed as if it is let.

3. Deductions from Income from House Property — Section 24

The annual value of house property as reduced by the following deductions is taxable under this head. This list of allowances is exhaustive. If any expenditure or loss is not covered under any of the following heads, it cannot be allowed as a deduction. If the deductions exceed the annual value of the property the loss can be set off against any income under any other head.

Section 24 provides only two types of deductions in place of earlier deductions, like deduction for repairs, interest, payment of ground rent, annual charge, insurance premium, etc. Thus, the newly substituted Section 24 provides the following two deductions only, namely:

(1) an amount equal to 30% of the annual value, and
(2) interest paid on capital borrowings for acquiring, constructing, repairing, renewing or reconstructing the property.

For a self-occupied house if the loan is taken as or after 1.4.1999 and the house is complete within three years from the end of the financial year in which the capital was borrowed, the deduction would be equal to the amount of interest or maximum upto Rs.1.5 lakh.

The deduction in respect of interest on borrowings for the property during construction will, however, be allowed as in the past over a five year period beginning with the year in which the property is so complete.

4. Unrealised Rent received subsequently to be charged to Tax —Section 25AA.

If unrealised rent is subsequently realised, it will be charged to tax as "income from house property" whether or not the assessee is the owner of that property in that previous year.

5. Taxation of arrears of rent in the year of receipt — Section 25B

If any arrears of rent other than what has already been taxed under Section 23, are received in a subsequent year, the same would be taxed in the year of receipt, whether property is owned by the assessee in the year of receipt or not. However, a deduction of sum equal to 30% of such amount of rent is allowed towards repairs and collection of rent.

PROBLEM NO. 7

Shyam Kumar receives rental income of ₹25,000 per month. House tax on the property is ₹20,000 per annum. By mistake he has not been able to pay house tax for the year ending on 31-3-2011. He has paid ₹15,000 to the society for maintenance of the flat. He also pays Fire Insurance premium of ₹6,000 per annum. Compute his Income from House Property for the year ending on 31-3-2012.

SOLUTION

Computation of the income from House Property of Shyam Kumar for the year ending on 31-3-2012:

	Rs.
Rent Received	3,00,000
Less: Municipal Taxes — No deduction will be allowed because the amount has not been paid:	— —
Annual Value	3,00,000

Contd . . .

	Rs.
Less:	
(1) Standard deduction for Repairs, etc. u/s 24 = 30% of A.V.	90,000
(2) Maintenance expenses — not separately allowed	— —
(3) Fire Insurance Premium — not separately allowed	— —
Income from House Property	2,10,000

6. Property Owned by Co-owners — Section 26

Where a property is owned by two or more persons and their respective shares are definite and ascertainable, such persons shall not, in respect of such property, be assessed as an association of persons, but the share of each such person in the income from the property as computed in accordance with Sections 22 to 25 (as described in paras 1 to 3 earlier) shall be includible in the total income. This Section would apply where a property is held by co-owners or tenants-in-common or where a block or flats are held on "ownership basis". Each co-owner would also be separately entitled to the concession under Section 23(2) in respect of the dwelling house (D.H.) for self-occupation as explained in para 7.

7. Self-Occupied House Property

A self-occupied house property would be completely exempt from income tax as per the amendment to Section 23(2)(a)(i). Where such a self-occupied house property is partly let-out and partly self-occupied, the annual value thereof will be determined as if the property had been let and will thereafter be reduced by that part of the annual value which is proportionate to the period during which the property is in occupation of the owner for the purpose of his own residence. Where the tax payer is the owner of more than one house property used for the purpose of his own residence, the annual value in respect of any one such house, which may be so specified by the assessee, would be taken such house, which may be so specified by the assessee, would be taken to be "Nil". Section 24 provides that in respect of such a house property whose annual value has been taken to be nil, no deduction under Section 24(1) in respect of repairs, would be allowed. The deduction in respect of loan taken for acquisition or construction of the self-occupied house, upto ₹1,50,000 p.a. would be allowed, so long as the acquisition or construction is completed within 3 years from the end of the financial year in which the capital was borrowed and the loan has been taken on or after 1-4-1999.

CHAPTER 7

Profits and Gains of Business or Profession

[SECTIONS 28 TO 44 OF I.T. ACT]

Introduction

This head of income is the most important of all because it attracts the highest amount of tax. Under this head tax is to be paid by an assessee on the profits and gains of a business or profession carried on by him. The net profits (i.e. gross incomings minus certain expenses) disclosed by an assessee are quite different from the taxable profits and gains to be ascertained in accordance with the Income Tax Act. While all the expenses claimed by an assessee in his profit and loss account are not deductible, all the income shown by him is also not taxable under this head. Therefore, it is very important for us to know and remember the expenses expressly allowed and disallowed by the IT Act in computing the taxable profits and gains from business or profession.

Chargeability under the Head "Profits and Gains of Business or Profession" — Section 28

"Business", as per Section 2(13) includes any trade, commerce or manufacture or any adventure or concern in the nature of trade, commerce or manufacture. "Profession" means an occupation involving manual or mental skill and it includes vocation also as per Section 2(36). The following income is chargeable to income tax under the head "profits and gains of business or profession" as per Section 28:

(i) the profits and gains of any business or profession which was carried on by the assessee at any time during the previous year;

(ii) certain compensation or other payment due to or received by a person managing a company, etc;

(iii) income derived by a trade, professional or similar association from specific services performed for its members;

(iiia) profits on sale of licence granted under the Imports (Control) Order, 1955, made under the Imports and Exports (Control) Act, 1947;

(iiib) cash assistance (by whatever name called) received or receivable by any person against exports under any scheme of the Government of India;

(iiic) any duty of customs or excise re-paid or repayable as drawback to any person against exports under the Customs and Central Excise Duties Drawback Rules, 1971;

(iv) the value of any benefit or perquisite, whether convertible into money or not, arising from business or the exercise of a profession;

(v) any interest, salary, bonus, commission or remuneration of a partner from a firm to the extent so allowed to the firm under Section 40(b).

(vi) any sum received under a Keyman Insurance Policy, with effect from 1.10.1996 [as per the Finance (No. 2) Act, 1996].

(vii) income from derivatives to be treated as business income.

Note: Speculation business is deemed to be distinct and separate from any other business.

Profits and Gains of Business — Section 28 (i)

The first type of income chargeable under this head is the "profits and gains" of any business carried out by the assessee for some time during the accounting year, though not necessarily throughout the year. Thus, if the business is discontinued before the commencement of the previous year the profits of the business received in the accounting year cannot be taxed on the principle that the source of income does not exist in the accounting year at all.

Compensation receipts would be taxable as business income. Likewise, bad debts recovered would also become taxable.

Allowable and Disallowable Deductions

General Principles

Section 29 provides that the income referred to in Section 28 shall be computed in accordance with the provisions contained in Sections 30 to 43A which provide for certain deductions. Besides, the specific deductions given in the Act, certain other losses and expenditure incidental to business are allowed as deduction from the gross profits.

Losses or Deductions Incidental to Trade — Section 28(i)

As stated above, it has been judicially recognised that an item of loss incidental to business may be allowed to be deducted in computing "profits and gains" under Section 28 (i) itself.

Deductions Expressly Allowed — Sections 30 to 37, 42, and 44 to 44D

The following are the important deductions are expressly allowed by the IT Act in computing chargeable business income under this head:

(i) Rent, rates, taxes, repairs and insurance of building [Section 30]. As per Finance Act, 2003 the amount paid for repairs shall not include the expenditure in the nature of capital expenditure.

(ii) Current repairs and insurance of machinery, plant and furniture [Section 31]. As per Finance Act, 2003 capital expenditure in the nature of current repairs shall not be allowed as a deduction.

(iii) Depreciation [Section 32] — Please see paras 18 to 23.

(iv) Expenditure on scientific research [Section 35] Any revenue expenditure laid out or expended by the assessee on scientific research related to the assessee's business is fully allowed as a deduction. Any sum paid to an approved scientific research association is also allowed deduction. Any sum paid to an approved college, etc. regarding statistical or social research related to the class of business is also allowed deduction. Besides, capital expenditure (Not being on land after 22-2-84) is also allowed full deduction. Weighted deduction @ 150% is also allowed in certain cases. The Finance Act, 2010 has increased the quantum of weighted deduction from 150% to 200%.

The Finance Act, 2008 has, w.e.f. the A.Y. 2009-10 made an amendment to Section 35(1)(iia) to provide that a weighted deduction of 125% of the amount paid by a person to a company to be used for scientific research would be allowed to such company. If it (i) is registered in India; (ii) has its main object the scientific research and development; (iii) is for the time being approved by the prescribed authority in a prescribed manner, and (iv) fulfils other prescribed conditions. The Finance Act, 2010 has increased the quantum of such deduction from 125% to 175%. The Finance Act, 2011 has, w.e.f. the A.Y. 2012-2013, provided for 200% weighted deduction for contribution made for approved scientific research programme, under Section 35 (2AA).

(v) Amortisation of certain preliminary expenses [Section 35D]. Where any resident person incurs any preliminary expenditure (as described below) before the commencement of business, or after the commencement of business in connection with the extension of his undertaking or in connection with the setting up a new unit, he shall be allowed a deduction in five years. The aggregate amount of such expenditure would be restricted to 5% of the cost of the project or capital employed in business of the company as against 2-1/2% earlier.

The following are the specimen of expenses which qualify for the aforesaid deduction:

(a) expenditure in connection with —
   (i) preparation of feasibility report;
   (ii) preparation of project report;
   (iii) conducting market survey or any other survey necessary for the business of the assessee;
   (iv) engineering service relating to the business of the assessee;

(b) Legal charges for drafting any agreement between the assessee and any other person for any purpose relating to the setting up or conduct of the business of the assessee, etc.

(vi) Insurance premium for stock and stores and Insurance premium paid by federal milk co-operative society [Section 36 (1) (i) & (ia)] & Health insurance premium [Section 36(1) (ib)].

(vii) Bonus and Commission to employees [Section 36 (1) (ii)].

(viii) Interest on borrowed capital [Section 36(1) (iii)].

(ix) Employer's contribution to a recognised provident fund, etc. [Section 36 (1) (iv)].

(x) Contribution towards an approved gratuity fund [Section 36 (1) (v)].

(xi) Contribution of employees to provident fund, etc. [Section 36 (1) (va)].

(xii) Bad debt [Section 36(1) (vii) and (36) (2)]. This will be allowed deduction in the year in which it is written off in accounts.

(xiii) Deduction of STT – Sec. 36(1)(xv) & 88E. No rebate u/s 88E would be allowed for STT from the A.Y. 2009-10. The amount of STT paid by the assessee during the year would be allowed as a deduction provided the income from STT transactions is included under the head "profits and gains of business or profession". This is by the Finance Act, 2008.

(xiv) Entertainment expenditure [Section 37(2), (2A)]. Expenditure in the nature of advertisement, travelling entertainment, hotel, guest house, etc., will be fully allowed.

(xv) Certain deductions to be allowed on actual payment [Section 43B]. It provides that in the case of tax payers maintaining the accounts on mercantile basis deduction for (a) any sum payable by way of tax, or duty, cess or fee, by whatever name called, whether or not such tax or duty, etc. is disputed), or (b) any contribution to any provident fund or superannuation fund or gratuity fund or any other fund maintained for the benefit or welfare of employees or (c) bonus or commission under Section 36(1) (ii) or (d) any interest to a public financial institution or a State Finance Corporation or a State Industrial Investment Corporation or (e) a scheduled bank (from the AY 1997-98) on loan and advances only shall be allowed only in the previous year in which such sum or contribution is actually paid during the previous year or in respect of sums is paid on or before the due date for filing the IT Return. The deduction for any sum payable by an employer in lieu of any leave at the credit of his employee would also be allowed only on actual payment basis.

(xvi) Deduction of Capital Expenditure on Specified Businesses [Section 35 AD]. — Full deduction even for capital expenditure (except expenditure on acquisition of land, goodwill and financial instrument) is allowed as a deduction only in respect of certain specified businesses like, cold chain facility, new two-star and above hotels, etc. Hospitals with 100 beds starting operations after 1.4.2010 would enjoy investment based deduction just like a hotel.

(xvii) Other expenditure [Section 37 (1)]. — This section provides for the deduction of any other expenditure laid out or expended wholly and exclusively for the purposes of the business in computing the business profits for the assessee provided that the expenditure is not of the nature described in Sections 30 to 36, or in the nature of capital expenditure or personal expenses of the assessee. However, illegal expenses will not be allowed any deduction as per Explanation to Section(37) (1) inserted by the Finance (No.2) Act, 1998 wef 1-4-1962. Expenses on Advertisement, Presents, Business Travelling will all be fully allowed.

Capital expenditure *versus* revenue expenditure

Under the Income-Tax Law capital expenditure is not allowed as a deduction. It is revenue expenditure alone which is allowed as a deduction.

Deductions Expressly Disallowed

There are certain types of allowances and deductions which are expressly prohibited by the Act. They are given below:

(i) Capital Expenditure

(ii) Illegal Expenses

(iii) Advertisement in Political Souvenir, etc.

(iv) Building, etc. not Exclusively Used for Business [Section38(2)].

(v) Interest, Royalty, etc. Payable Outside India [Section 40(a)(i)].
As per Finance Act, 2003 if tax has not been deducted or after deduction has not been paid will not be allowed.

(vi) Interest, Salary etc., to a Partner [Section 40(b)]

Payment of salary and interest to partners in excess of the specified limit, explained in detail in Chapter XIV, is to be disallowed.

(vii) Restrictions on the Deduction of Expenses or Payments in Certain Circumstances [Section 40A(2)]

Where any expenditure is incurred in a business for which payment has been or is to be made to the specified categories of persons (broadly the tax payer's relatives and associate concerns) the expenditure to the extent it is considered to be excessive or unreasonable will not be allowed as a deduction in computing the profits of the business. The reasonableness of any expenditure is to be judged having regard to the fair market value of the goods, services or facilities for which the payment is made or the legitimate needs of the business or the benefit derived by the assessee from the expenditure.

(viii) Expenditure Exceeding ₹20,000 at a Time to be made by Crossed Bank Cheque or Draft [Section 40A(3)]

A provision has been made for the disallowance of 100% expenditure in business or profession by an assessee for which payment is made in an amount exceeding ₹20,000 unless the payment is made on account payee cheque or on account payee bank draft except in certain prescribed circumstances, as per the Finance Act, 2007.

Where the aggregate payments of business expenditure to a person in a day, otherwise than a/c payee cheque or bank draft exceeds ₹20,000, the whole of such amount would be disallowed in computing the business income of the tax payer. This is so made by the Finance Act, 2008 w.e.f. the A.Y. 2009-10. The Finance (No. 2) Act. 2009 has, w.e.f. 1-10-2009 provided for the increased limit of ₹35,000 in case of payment made for plying, hiring or leasing goods carriages.

(ix) Disallowance of Deduction in Respect of Provision for Payment of Gratuity to Employees — [Section 40A (7)]

No deduction will be allowed in the computation of profits and gains of a business or profession in respect of any reserve created or provision made for the payment of gratuity to the employees on retirement or on termination of employment for any reason.

(x) Contributions to Employees Welfare Funds, etc. [Section 40A(9), 10 and 11]

No deduction would be allowed in respect of any sum paid by the assessee as an employer towards the setting up or formation of, or as contribution to any fund, trust, company, association of persons, body of individuals, society registered under the Societies Registration Act, 1860 or other institution for any purpose, subject to certain conditions.

(xi) Enforcing Compliance of Provisions of TDS — Section 40(a)(ia)

Certain payments like interest, commission or brokerage, fees for professional services or fees for technical services to residents and payments to a contractor or sub-contractor for carrying out any work, on which tax not been deducted at source or has not been paid in time would be disallowed. However, the deduction would be allowed later in computing the income of the previous year in which such tax has been paid. This amendment is operative on and from the A.Y. 2005-06.

As per the Taxation Laws (Amendment) Act, 2005 if TDS is not deduction or after deduction is not paid in respect of rent and royalty, then the same would not be allowed as a deduction.

The Finance Act, 2008 has amended Section 40(a)(ia) to provide that the disallowance in respect of payment for rent, royalty, etc. will not be made in the case of a deductor for the expenditure incurred in the month of March if the TDS on such an expenditure had been paid before the date of filing of the return. Thus, the tax payers will now get a time period of 6 months for depositing TDS relatable to payments in the month of March to escape the disallowance of the expenditure under Section 40(a)(ia) of the Income Tax Act. This amendment has been given retrospective effect from the A.Y. 2005-06.

As per the Finance Act, 2010 the tax deduction at source but not paid during the financial year would be allowed deduction even if the same is paid by the last date of filing the income-tax return.

Other Disallowable Expenditure

In para 12 we have mentioned the case of disallowable deductions as specifically provided in the Act. There are several types of expenditure which though not capital in nature or expressly disallowed by the Act may not be wholly allowed under Section 37(1) on the ground that they are not wholly and exclusively incurred for purposes of the business, e.g. Contribution to a political party, etc.

PROBLEM No. 8

Shyam Lal has incurred following expenses for his business; please state whether they would be allowed or not:—

1. Bribe paid in Govr. department: ₹25,000.
2. Bad Debts from a Business party: ₹12, 800
3. Air Travel to Simla with family: ₹16, 000
4. Interest on business loan: ₹38, 000

SOLUTION

1. Bribe paid is illegal business expenditure, hence not allowed.
2. Bad debts will be allowed as a deduction.
3. Air travel expenses not to be allowed because it is for personal trip.
4. Interest on business loan would be allowed deduction.

Method of Accounting [Section 145(1)]

The profits and gains of business or profession have to be computed in accordance with either cash or merchantile system of accounting regularly employed by the assessee. The choice of the method of accounting to be followed regularly lies with the assessee. Once the assessee adopts a method of accounting for recording his business transactions he has to regularly follow the same. The following are the two methods of accounting so recognised from AY 1997-98:

(i) Cash method of accounting; and
(ii) Mercantile method of accounting;

Compulsory Maintenance of Books of Account by Professionals and Businessmen [Section 44AA]

Every person carrying on legal, medical, engineering, or architectural profession or the profession of accountancy or technical consultancy or interior decoration or any other notified profession would be required to keep and maintain such books of account and other documents as to enable the Assessing Officer to compute his total income. However, every person carrying on any other business or profession would also be required to maintain such books of account and other documents as may enable the AO to compute his total income under the Act provided the following conditions as amended from the AY 1999-2000 are fulfilled, namely:

(i) If his income from business or profession exceeds ₹1,20,000 or his total sales, turnover or gross receipts, as the case may be, in business or profession exceed or exceeds ₹10 lakh in any one of the three years immediately preceding the previous year.

(ii) Where the business or profession is newly set up in any previous year and if his income from profession or business is likely to exceed ₹1,20,000 or his total sales, turnover or gross receipts, as the case may be in the business or business are or is likely to exceed ₹10 lakh during such year.

Estimated Income Method for Contractors, Business, etc.— Section 44 AD

The income of all assessees whose gross receipts from the business of civil construction or supply of labour for civil construction work do not exceed ₹60 lakh will be estimated at his option at 8% of the gross receipts paid or payable. All deductions including depreciation will be deemed to be allowed. Such assessees will not be required to compulsorily maintain books of account. If a person wants to be assessed at a lower rate, then he shall maintain accounts and get the same audited. This section has been substituted by a new section from the A. Y. 2011-12 to provide for the computation of the profits and gains of any business @ 8% of gross turn over or receipts which do not exceed ₹60 lakh.

Estimated Income Method for Truck Owners, etc. — Section 44 AE

In respect of the income from the business of plying, hiring or leasing trucks owned by a tax payer, an optional estimated scheme will be applicable whereby the income from each heavy goods vehicle, will be estimated at ₹3,500 p.m. and for owners of light goods vehicles it will be ₹3,150 p.m. per vehicle. From the A.Y. 2011-12 the aforesaid sum would be ₹5,000 p.m. and ₹4,500 p.m. respectively. The scheme applies to persons owning not more than 10 trucks at any time during the year. All deductions, including depreciation, will be deemed to have been already allowed. It would not be necessary to maintain books of account. If a person wants to be assessed at a lower rate, then he shall maintain accounts and get the same audited.

Estimated Income Scheme for Computing Profits and Gains of Retail Traders — Section 44AF

The Finance Act, 1997 introduced a new scheme for computing profits and gains of such business presumptively at five per cent of the gross receipts. This would be applicable in the case of retail traders whose sales or turnover does not exceed ₹40 lakh. Under this scheme a retail trader would be free to estimate his turnover at any figure upto ₹40 lakh and be taxed on the total income computed at 5% thereon. For example, if a retail trader estimates his sales to be ₹23 lakh, for the Financial Year 2007-2008, relevant to the AY 2008-2009, this profits and gains presumptively estimated under Section 44AF would be ₹1,15,000 on which he would be required to pay income tax of ₹500 only. For the A.Y. 2009-10 no tax would be payable as it is below the exemption limit. The retail trader will not be required to maintain books of account. However, if he wishes to be assessed at a lower figure, he would be required to prove the income so returned by him and he would also be required to compulsorily maintain books of account and be subject to tax audit. This section would not apply from the A. Y. 2011-12.

Special Provision for Computing Profits and Gains of Business on Presumptive Basis — Section 44AD

On and from the Assessment Year 2011-2012 special provision is now existing in terms of Section 44AD for computing profit on presumptive basis in respect of any type of plying. hiring or leasing of vehicles. A sum of 8% of the total turnover would be treated as the income from such business. The total turnover or gross receipts should not exceed ₹60 lakh.

Audit of Accounts of Certain Persons Carrying on Business or Profession — Section 44AB

It is obligatory for a person carrying on business to get the accounts audited by an "accountant" within the meaning of Section 288 of the IT Act if the total sales or gross receipts for the financial year 2010-2011 exceed ₹60 lakh. Similarly, a person carrying on profession will have to get the accounts audited in the same manner if the gross receipts for the relevant previous year exceed ₹15 lakh. Besides, tax audit is also compulsory for those assessees who do not wish to pay tax as per the estimated income scheme of Sections 44AD, 44AE or 44AF. Failure to do so will entail a penalty of sum calculated at 1/2% of the total sales or gross receipts, as the case may be, subject to a maximum of ₹1,50,000 lakh under Section 271B from the A.Y. 2011-2012.

Valuation of Stock

The valuation of stock-in-hand at the close of the accounting year is an important aspect of the method of accounting employed. Correct profits cannot be determined unless the unsold stock-in-trade of the assessee is properly valued by the assessee.

The value of the closing stock of the business must be entered, at the option of the assessee, either at the cost price or market price, or the lower of the two.

A.O's Powers to Estimate Profit or Make Additions — Section 145(3)

Section 145 gives wide powers to the AO in the matter of estimating the profits of an assessee according to the best of his judgment. Such a power can be exercised by him in any of the following circumstances from the AY 1997-98:

(a) Where he is not satisfied about the correctness or the completeness of the accounts of the assessee — Section 145(3).
(b) Where no method of accounting or the accounting standards have been regularly followed by the assessee — Section 145(3).

The AO shall compute the profits upon such basis and such manner as he may determine in the manner provided in Section 144, i.e. to the best of his judgment as per Section 145 (3).

Taxation of non-compete fees and exclusive rights — Section 28(va)

Any sum received or receivable in cash or in kind under an agreement for not carrying out activity in relation to any business or not to share any know-how, patent, copyright, trade-mark, licence, franchise or any other business or commercial right of similar nature or information or technique, etc. would be taxable under the head "Profits and gains of business or profession".

Depreciation, etc.

Conditions for the Grant of Depreciation Allowance — Sections 32 and 34

The general rule under the Income Tax Act is to charge tax on profits or income without making any allowance for deduction in respect of the exhaustion or diminution in the value of capital. To this principle an exception is found in Section 32 under which a deduction is allowed to an assessee in respect of the normal depreciation on building, machinery, plant or furniture wholly or partly owned by the assessee as also on intangible assets. Depreciation is mandatory from the A.Y. 2002-2003.

Depreciation on Intangible Assets — Sections 2(11), 32, 35A & 35AB

Depreciation would now be available on intangible assets which are owned wholly or partly by the assessee and are used by such assessee for the purpose of his business or profession. The intangible assets, such as know-how, patent rights, copyrights, trade marks, licences, franchises or any other business or commercial rights of the assessee will form a separate block of assets and depreciation at 25% will be allowed on the written down value at the end of the financial year.

Block of Assets

As per Section 2 (11) "Block of Assets" means a group of assets falling within a class of assets, being buildings, machinery, plant or furniture in respect of which the same percentage of depreciation is prescribed, as per the revised Appendix I to the Income Tax Rules.

For example, plant and machinery — like motor buses, certain air pollution control equipments, motor lorries and motor taxies for hire — are entitled to a depreciation of 40%. upto the A.Y. 2005-2006 only and at the rate of 30% on and from the A.Y. 2006-07. Hence, these are grouped together under one block of assets for the purpose of calculating depreciation. Similarly, where a tax-payer owns different items of furniture and fittings like chairs, tables, almirahs, they are classified under the general heading of furniture and fittings entitled to depreciation @ 15% upto the A.Y. 2005-06 only and at the rate of 10% on and from the A.Y. 2006-2007.

New Rates of Depreciation

As per the revised depreciation rules the tangible assets have been classified under the following four categories of block of assets, namely:

(i) Buildings;
(ii) Furniture and fittings;
(iii) Machinery and plant; and
(iv) Ships.

Under each of the aforesaid four broad types of assets there are sub-divisions indicating the different block of assets for which a common single rate of depreciation, as a percentage of the written down value, would be allowed.

For example, office and factory buildings would generally be entitled to a depreciation @10%. In respect of furniture and fittings the 15% general rate of depreciation upto the A.Y. 2005-06 only and at the rate of 30% on and from the A.Y. 2006-2007. Assets used for less than 180 days are entitled to 50% of the prescribed rates of depreciation.

All types of plant and machinery have been divided into different block of assets, entitled to four rates of depreciation, namely, 20%, 25%, 40%, 60%, 80% and 100%. The general rate of depreciation on plant & machinery was 25% while on computers it was 60%.

As per the Income Tax (Sixth Amendment) Rules 2005 w.e.f. the Assessment Year 2006-07 new depreciation rates have been prescribed. The general new rates of depreciation are 15% for plant and machinery, 10% for furniture, 15% for motor cars and 60% for computers.

Written-down Value (WDV)

Depreciation allowance is allowed as per the new rates of depreciation as a percentage of the written down value. The written down value of any block of assets, i.e. the different items of assets under a particular category entitled to the same rate of depreciation, would be the aggregate of the written down value of all the assets falling within that block of assets at the beginning of the previous year plus the actual cost of any assets falling within the block acquired during the previous year, as reduced by the moneys payable in respect of any assets within the block which is sold, etc. during that previous year. Thus, no separate balancing allowance or charge would be calculated in future.

Short-term Capital Gains

It may sometimes happen that the sale proceeds of any asset or all assets of a particular block of assets may exceed the written down value of that block of assets. In that case the difference between the sale value and the written down value would be deemed to be short-term capital gains. Likewise, if all the assets comprising a block of assets are sold and there is no asset left in the relevant block of assets at the end of the year, then under the provisions of Section 50(2) of the Income Tax Act the difference between the written down value and the sale proceeds received in respect of the assets from that block sold during the year would be deemed to be short-term capital loss.

PROBLEM No. 9

The following particulars for depreciation purposes are furnished by a company for the accounting year ended 31st March, 2012:

	₹	₹
Factory Building:		
W.D.V on 1-4-2011	25,00,000	
Addition on 1-4-2011	10,00,000	35,00,000
Machinery (Dep. rate 15%)		
W.D.V. on 1-4-2011	60,00,000	
New Addition on 9-6-2011	12,00,000	72,00,000
Furniture (Dep. rate 10%)		
W.D.V. on 1-4-2011	3,00,000	
Addition on 1-7-2011	1,00,000	4,00,000

Calculate the amount of depreciation admissible for the assessment year 2012-2013 and the written down value on 1st April, 2012.

SOLUTION

The amount of depreciation allowable for the assessment year 2012-2013 is as under:

	₹	₹	₹
Factory Buildings:			
Depreciation at 10% on	35,00,000	—	3,50,000
Written down value on			
1-4-2012 will be	35,00,000		
Less: depreciation	3,50,000		
	31,50,000		
Machinery:			
Normal Depreciation at 15% on	60,00,000	9,00,000	
-do- " on	12,00,000	1,80,000	10,80,000
Written down value			
on 1-4-2012 will be	72,00,000	—	—
Less: Normal depreciation	10,80,000		
	61,20,000		
Furniture:			
Depreciation at 10% on	3,00,000	30,000	
Depreciation at 10% on	1,00,000	10,000	40,000
Written down value on			
1-4-2012 will be	4,00,000		
Less: Depreciation	40,000		
	3,60,000		
Total Depreciation			14,70,000

Additional Depreciation on New Machinery and Plant — Section 32

As per the Finance Act, 2002 deduction would be allowed of a further 15% of the actual cost of new machinery or plant acquired and installed after 31.3.2002 (i) in the case of a new industrial undertaking in the previous year in which it begins to manufacture or produce any article or thing; or (b) in the case of an existing industrial undertaking in the previous year in which it achieves substantial expansion by way of increase in the installed capacity (existing on the last day of the previous year commencing on or after 31.3.2002) by not less than 25% The installed capacity means the capacity of production as on 31.3.2002. As per the Finance Act, 2005, w.e.f. the A.Y. 2006-07 the rate of additional depreciation on new plant and machinery would be 20%.

Reduction in the limit for Installed Capacity for Additional Depreciation — Section 32(1)(iia)

The limit for increase in installed capacity for additional depreciation has been reduced from 25% to 10% only. This amendment is operative for the A.Y. 2005-06, as per the Finance (No. 2) Act, 2004.

As per the Finance Act, 2005 w.e.f. the A.Y. 2006-2007 the requirement of creating a minimum increase of 10% of installed capacity for availing the initial or additional depreciation is eliminated.

The depreciation on Wind Mills installed after 1-4-2012 will be 15% per annum.

CHAPTER 8

Capital Gains

(SECTIONS 45 TO 55A OF I.T. ACT)

1. Capital Gains on Transfer of Capital Asset — Section 45 (1)

Section 45 (1) provides that tax shall be payable by an assessee under the head "Capital Gains" in respect of any profits arising from the transfer, i.e., sale, exchange, relinquishment of a capital asset, etc. Such profit shall be deemed to be income of the previous year in which the sale, exchange, relinquishment, etc. took place.

The duration of holding a capital asset and the various expenses and other deductions to be claimed for arriving at the final quantum of taxable capital gains have a direct bearing on the incidence of income tax in relation to the capital gains in respect of transfer of the capital assets. There are certain transactions which are not regarded as "transfer" and these are outside the orbit of capital gains tax. Similarly, there are certain rules laid down for determining the actual cost of a capital asset which is to be deducted in arriving at the net taxable capital gains. There are certain types of capital gains which are not as a result of some actual transfer of capital asset but which are "deemed" as such under the provisions of Section 45, sub-section (2), (3), (4), (5) and (6) namely:

(a) Profit and gain from a capital asset which is converted into stock in trade.

(b) Fair market value of capital asset distributed by a partnership firm on dissolution, and

(c) On compulsory acquisition by law, etc.

2. What is a capital asset?

For the purposes of bringing to tax any gain under the head "capital gain", the item transferred must be a capital asset. Hence its definition becomes very important. As per Section 2(14) of the IT Act, 1961 it is defined as property of any kind held by an assessee whether or not connected with his business or profession, but not including stock-in-trade, personal effects and agricultural land outside municipality or within 8 km. from municipality, Gold Deposit Bonds.

The most important item that should be noted in this regard is "personal effects" like silver utensils, wearing apparel, etc. which are not treated as capital assets.

As per the Finance Act, 2005 the gain arising on Zero Coupon Bond will be treated as capital gain.

The scope of "capital assets" is widened so as to exclude from the meaning of "personal effects", archaeological collections, drawings, paintings, sculptures or any work of art, in addition to jewellery, so as to attract capital gains tax on their transfer. This amendment is made by the Finance Act, 2007 and is effective from the A.Y. 2008-2009.

3. Long-term and Short-term Capital Gains

Capital assets are of two types: long-term capital assets and short-term capital assets. Under Section 2(42A) a "short-term capital" asset means a capital asset held by an assessee for not more than 36 months immediately preceding the date of its transfer. However, in the case of a share held in a company or any other security listed in a recognised stock exchange in India or a unit of UTI or a unit of an approved mutual fund, the words "12 months" would be substituted for the words "36 months". Where any capital asset is held by an assessee in the case of a share held in a company in liquidation, the period subsequent to the date on which the company goes into liquidation would be excluded. In the case of a capital asset which becomes the property of the assessee, say, by gift or by will or by partition of an HUF, etc., the period for which the asset was held by the previous owner referred in Section 49(1) would also be included. Thus the amount received on the renunciation of right share would normally be taxable as a short-term capital gain. As regards bonus shares, the cost price would be treated as "nil". The asset which is not a short-term capital asset is regarded as a long-term capital asset which results in long-term capital gains, on its transfer.

4. Indexation of Long-term Capital Gains

The two deductions which are allowed for computing the capital gains under Section 48 from the full value of the consideration received or accruing as a result of the transfer of the capital asset are the following:

(i) Expenditure incurred wholly and exclusively in connection with such transfer; and

(ii) The cost of acquisition of the asset and the cost of any improvement thereof.

The second proviso to Section 48 provides that in the case of long-term capital gain arising from the long-term capital asset for "indexed cost of acquisition" and "indexed cost of any improvement" would be deducted. Hence, it is absolutely necessary for taxpayers to know the meaning of the expression "indexed cost of acquisition". Clause(iii) of the Explanation to Section 48 defines this expression as under:

"Indexed cost of Acquisition" means an amount which bears to the cost of acquisition the same proportion as Cost Inflation Index for the year in which the asset is transferred bears to the Cost Inflation Index the first year in which the asset was held by the assessee or for the beginning on 1-4-1981, whichever is later.

The expression "Indexed Cost of any improvement" as per clause (iv) of the Explanation to Section 48 is defined as under:

"Indexed cost of any improvement" means an amount which bears to cost of improvement the same proportion as Cost Inflation Index the year in which the asset is transferred bears to the Cost Inflation for the year in which the improvement to the asset took place.

Thus, for calculating the taxable amount of long-term capital gains, a tax payer can now suitably index the cost of acquisition as also the cost of any improvement with reference to the Cost Inflation Index which is notified each year by the Government. Cost Inflation Index would be available to all tax payers on all types of assets. However, the concept of Cost Inflation Index would not be applicable on Bonds and Debentures.

5. Cost Inflation Index

The Cost Inflation Index has been notified by the Central Government. It is reproduced below for the sake of guidance for all the assessees having long-term capital gains:

Sl. No.	Financial Year	Cost Inflation Index	Sl. No.	Financial Year	Cost Inflation Index
(1)	(2)	(3)	(1)	(2)	(3)
1.	1981-1982	100	17.	1997-1998	331
2.	1982-1983	109	18.	1998-1999	351
3.	1983-1984	116	19.	1999-2000	389
4.	1984-1985	125	20.	2000-2001	406
5.	1985-1986	133	21.	2001-2002	426
6.	1986-1987	140	22.	2002-2003	447
7.	1987-1988	150	23.	2003-2004	463
8.	1988-1989	161	24.	2004-2005	480
9.	1989-1990	172	25.	2005-2006	497
10.	1990-1991	182	26.	2006-2007	519
11.	1991- 1992	199	27.	2007-2008	551
12.	1992-1993	223	28.	2008-2009	582
13.	1993-1994	244	29.	2009-2010	632
14.	1994-1995	259	30.	2010-2011	711
15.	1995-1996	281	31.	2011-2012	785
16.	1996-1997	305			

6. Cost of Acquisition for Certain Modes of Acquisition of a Capital Asset

It is provided in Section 49(1) of the Income Tax Act that where the capital asset became the property of the assessee on any distribution of assets on the total or partial partition of an HUF; or under a gift or will; or (a) by succession, inheritance or devolution, or on distribution of assets on dissolution then the cost of acquisition of the asset shall be deemed to be the cost for which the previous owner of the property acquired it, as increased by the cost of any improvement of the asset or borne by any of the previous owner or the assessee, as the case may be.

The Finance (No.2) Act, 2009 further provides that where the capital gain arises from the transfer of a property the value of which was subjected to income-tax as per Section 56, then the cost of acquisition of such property shall be deemed to be the value which has been taken into account for the purpose of Section 56.

7. Cost of Acquisition in the case of Depreciable Assets and Computing Short-term Capital Gains

As per Section 50 of the Income Tax Act it is provided that where the capital asset is an asset forming part of a block of assets in respect of which depreciation has been allowed under this Act, the provisions of Sections 48 and 49 shall be subject to the following modifications:

(1) Where the full value of the consideration received or accruing as a result of the transfer of the asset, together with the full value of such consideration received or accruing as a result of the transfer of any other capital asset falling within the block of assets during the previous year, exceeds the aggregate of the following amounts, namely:

(i) expenditure incurred wholly and exclusively in connection with such transfer or transfers;
(ii) the written-down value of the block of assets at the beginning of the previous year; and
(iii) the actual cost of any asset falling within the block of assets acquired during the previous year, such excess shall be deemed to

be the capital gains arising from the transfer of short-term capital assets;

(2) Where any block of assets ceases to exist as such, for the reason that all the assets in the block are transferred during the previous year, the cost of acquisition of the block of assets shall be the written-down value of the block of assets at the beginning of the previous year as increased by the actual cost of any asset falling within that block of assets, acquired by the assessee during the previous year and the income received or accruing as a result of such transfers or transfer, shall be deemed to be the capital gains from the transfer of short-term capital assets.

8. Cost of Acquisition in Certain Other Cases

For the purposes of determining the cost of acquisition for Sections 48 and 49 in relation to a capital asset, Section 55(2) provides certain special rules for this purpose. The cost of acquisition in a case where the capital asset became the property of the assessee before 1-4-1981,means the cost of acquisition of the asset to the assessee or the fair market value of the asset on 1-4-1981, at the option of the assessee; or (ii) where the capital asset became the property of the assessee by any of the modes specified in Section 49(1), and the capital asset became the property of the previous owner before 1-4-1981, means the cost of capital asset to the previous owner of the fair market value of the asset as on 1-4-1981, at the option of the assessee.

It is provided that the cost of acquisition of the right to manufacture, produce or process any article or thing would be "nil" as in the case of goodwill and tenancy rights. Hence, the entire receipts on the extinguishment of the right to manufacture, produce or process any article or thing for a consideration will be liable to the capital gains tax.

9. The Meaning of "Cost of any Improvement"

We have seen above that the "Cost of any Improvement" to a capital asset is deductible in computing the net taxable capital gains. The expression "Cost of any Improvement" as per Section 55(1)(b) of the Income Tax Act in relation to a capital asset, means

(1) in relation to goodwill — nil, and

(2) in relation to any other capital asset, — (i) where the capital asset became the property of the previous owner or the assessee before 1-4-1981, and the fair market value of the asset on that dateis taken as the cost of acquisition at the option of the assessee, means all expenditure incurred in making any additions or alterations to the capitalasset on or after "the said date" by the previous owner or the assessee;and (ii) in any other case, means all expenditure of a capital nature incurred in makingany additions or alterations to the capital asset by the assessee after it became his property, and, where the capital asset became the property of the assessee by any of the modes, specified in Section 49(1) by the previous owner, but does not include any expenditure which is deductible incomputing the income chargeable under any other head.

10. What is a Transfer?

As per Section 2(47) "transfer" in relation to a capital asset includes:

(i) sale, exchange or relinquishment of the asset, or

(ii) the extinguishment of any right therein, or

(iii) the compulsory acquisition thereof under any law, or

(iv) in a case, where the asset is converted by the owner thereof into or is treated by him as stock-in-trade of a business carried on by him, such conversion or treatment, or

(v) any transaction involving the allowing of the possession of any immovable property to be taken or retained in part performance of a contract of the nature referred to in Section 53A of the Transfer of Property Act, 1882, or

(vi) any transaction, whether by way of becoming a member of, or acquiring shares in aco-operative society, company or other AOP or by way of an agreement or any arrangement or in any other manner whatsoever which is effected by transferring or enabling enjoyment of, any immovable property.

11. Transactions not regarded as "Transfers"

Not every kind of transfer of a capital asset subjects the gains therefrom to capital gains tax. This is because there are certain kinds of transfers which are not regarded as covered under the charging Section 45 and consequently any capital gains made by an assessee as a result of transfer of a capital asset in those cases would be wholly exempt from tax. The following are some of the important types of such transfers which are not regarded as "transfers" for the purposes of capital gains tax as per Section 47:

(i) Any distribution of capital asset on the total or partial partition of a Hindu Undivided Family ;

(ii) Any distribution of capital asset on the dissolution of a firm, body of individuals or other association of persons;

(iii) Any transfer of a capital asset under a gift or will or an irrevocable trust;

(iv) Conversion of partnership firm to a company on fulfilment of certain conditions.

(vi) Demergers and amalgamations

(vii) Transfer of a capital asset in a transaction of reverse mortgage (from the A.Y. 2008-09).

As per the Finance Act, 2003 as per new Section 10(36) w.e.f. the financial year 2003-04 any income arising from transfer of a long-term capital asset being the equity shares of B.S.E. 500 Index of Mumbai Stock Exchange would be exempt provided the same are acquired during the period 1-3-2003 to 28-2-2004. Likewise, shares purchased under new public issue during the period 1-3-2003 o 28-2-2004 would also not be liable to any capital gains if sold after 12 months.

12. Exemption of Long-term Capital Gains on Investment in House Property

The incentive by way of complete income tax exemption in respect of capital gain is contained in Section 54. Thus, if an investor transfers his residential house or a part thereof and makes a long-term capital gain, (relating to a house property which was acquired over three years ago) and if the entire long-term capital gain is invested in the purchase of a residential house property within one year in anticipation of the transfer or within two years of the transfer or if the house property is constructed within three years of the transfer and the entire long-term capital gain is invested in the acquisition of such residential house property, the entire long-term capital gain in respect of the transfer of the first residential house property would be fully exempt from income tax. Where, however, the entire long-term capital gain is not so utilised or a part thereof is so invested, then only the proportional amount of long-term capital gain would be so exempt.

A procedural requirement about the claim of exemption of long-term capital gains should also be understood clearly. If by the last date of the voluntary filing of Income tax Return under Section 139(1), the entire long-term capital gain is not so utilised, then it should be deposited with a bank under a Capital Gains A/c Scheme and the receipt thereof should be enclosed with the IT return. Such amount of capital gain not so utilised which is deposited with the bank under the scheme can be withdrawn as and when required.

13. Exemption of Long-term Capital Gains regarding any Capital Asset on Investment in a Residential House

Another income tax exemption which can be enjoyed by an investor on investment in residential house property can be secured under Section 54F. Thus, where an investor has a long-term capital gain on the transfer of any capital asset (other than a residential house) like shares, a plot of land, commercial assets, commercial house property, jewellery, etc., then he can secure complete income tax exemption on the long-term capital gain in respect of the sale of the capital asset if the entire net sale proceeds thereof are invested in the acquisition of a residential house or a part either by purchase or construction. Thus, the entire net sale proceeds should be invested within one year of the transfer in advance or within two years from the date of transfer in the purchase of a residential house property or the sale proceeds may be invested within three years in the construction of a residential house property. However, there is one more condition, which is very important and which must be ensured by every taxpayer. This benefit of exemption is available only where the taxpayer does not own any residential house as on the date of the transfer of the capital asset. Further, the lock-in period for the new residential house so acquired is three years. Where the entire sale proceeds of any capital asset are not so invested in the residential house property on or before the last date of voluntary filing of the income tax return, then the same procedural requirement about the investment of the money in a separate bank account in a Capital Gain A/c Scheme, as explained earlier, for the purposes of Section 54 is equally applicable for Section 54F.

14. Exemption of Capital Gains in Agricultural Land — Section 54B

Where the capital gains, both short-term and long-term, arise from the transfer of a capital asset, being land which, in the two years immediately preceding the date on which the transfer took place, was being used by the assessee or a parent of his for agricultural purposes, and the assessee has, within a period of 2 years after that date, purchased any other land for being used for agricultural purposes, then capital gains tax would not be charged.

15. Exemption of Capital Gains from the Acquisition of Industrial Undertakings

Under the provisions of Section 54D there is an exemption provided in the case of a person owning an industrial undertaking, whether land or building used by him for the purposes of business or the industrial undertaking is compulsorily acquired.

16. Income Tax Rates on Long-term Capital Gains

The rates of long-term capital gains are contained in Section 112. Broadly speaking, the rate of income tax payable on long-term capital gains after indexed cost of improvement taking into account the indexed cost of acquisition under Section 48 would be 20% in the case of individuals, HUFs, companies, firms and AOPs.

As a result of the application of the indexed cost of acquisition as also the indexed cost of improvement by taking into account the Cost Inflation Index, the effective rate of tax on the long-term capital gains can work out to a very low figure of about 9% only and, in some cases where the asset was acquired prior to 1 April 1981, to an even lower percentage.

17. Carry-forward of Loss

Due to the application of cost inflation index, there could be a loss under the head capital gains then the same would be allowed to be carried forward for set off against capital gains in future for a period of 8 years. However, the long-term capital gain can be adjusted only against long-term capital gain of the year or else it can carry forward for subsequent 8 years but only against long-term capital gains.

18. Modified exemption under Section 54

Due to the new method of calculating the taxable long-term capital gains, there will be a change in the amount to be invested for getting complete exemption from income tax under Section 54. Section 54 provides that in case of a long-term capital gain relating to a residential house, the entire long-term capital gain can be tax-free if the amount of the long-term capital gains is invested in the purchase or construction of another residential house within a period of 1, 2 and 3 years, as the case may be. In such a case, it is not the full amount of the actual gain but the taxable capital gain as calculated after giving effect to the deduction for the Cost Inflation Index under Section 48 which is to be invested. However, if there is a sale of capital asset not being a residential house and the assessee wants an exemption under Section 54F by investing in a residential house, then the entire sale consideration will have to be invested.

19. Exemption of Long-term Capital Gains on Investment in Bonds

As per Section 54EC exemption in respect of long-term capital gains in the hands of any assessee is available on inveshment in certain bonds. The exemption from tax on long-term capital gains would be to the extent of investment in these bonds with a cap of ₹50 lakh in a financial year. These bonds would have a lock-in period of three years.

The bonds of NHAI and REC alone would qualify for exemption of long-term capital gains under Section 54EC.

20. Exemption of Long-term Capital Gains on Securities and Units on Investment in Primary Issues

In terms of Section 54 ED the long-term capital gains arising from the transfer of listed securities or units of a Mutual Fund or the UTI would be exempt from tax if the gain is invested in equity shares forming part of an eligible issue of capital made by a public company and offered for subscription to public. There would be a lock-in period of one year and if the newly acquired shares are sold or transferred during this period, the capital gains from the original asset will be charged to tax in the year of sale or transfer. This provision has now been deleted by the Finance Act, 2006.

21. Computation of Capital Gains in Real Estate Transactions

Section 50C provides that where the consideration declared to be received or accruing as a result of the transfer of land or building or both is less than the value adopted or assessed by any authority of the State Government for the purpose of payment of stamp duty in respect of such transfer, the value so adopted or assessed would be deemed to be the full value of the consideration, and the capital gains would be computed accordingly under Section 48 of the I.T. Act. From 1-10-2009 this section would also apply to "assessable" value.

22. Taxation of Long-term Capital Gains on Equity Shares and Units of Equity-oriented Mutual Funds

As a result of insertion of Section 10(38) by the Finance (No. 2) Act, 2004 income arising from the transfer of a long-term capital asset being equity shares as also units of equity-oriented mutual funds would be exempted from the purview of long-term capital gains.

This exemption is, however, not applicable on capital gains arising on sale of any type of equity share. It is very clearly mentioned that the exemption from tax in respect of such long-term capital gains would be available only when the transaction relating to sale of equity share or units of equity-oriented is entered into on or after the 1st October 2004. Another condition to avail this exemption is that such transaction is chargeable to Securities Transaction Tax (STT). If a person sells shares of a listed company directly to a friend without routing it through a stock broker, then the benefits of exemption of long-term capital gains on such sale of equity shares would not be available.

Similarly, if the shares of a private limited company are sold after holding them for more than 12 months, then the above mentioned benefits would not be available because such shares are not sold through the stock broker and thus the transaction is not subjected to STT. Therefore, in view of the fact that the shares of a Private Limited Company are not chargeable to STT, the same would not enjoy any tax benefits.

If the sale of units of an equity-oriented fund results into a long-term capital gains, it would also be tax free if the said transaction is chargeable to STT.

It has been clarified that "equity-oriented fund" would mean a fund where the investible funds are invested in equity shares of domestic companies to the extent of more than 50% of total corpus of the fund. As per the Finance Act, 2006 the percentage of investment has to be more than 65%. Moreover, such a fund should have been set up as a scheme of a mutual fund in terms of Section 23D of the Income-tax Act, 1961. It has also clarified that the percentage of equity share holding of the fund shall be computed as the annual average of its average monthly holding of equity based on opening and closing figures. Thus, where a mutual fund has exposure to equity investment of, say, only 15% to 25%, then the above mentioned benefit would not be available.

23 Taxation of Short-term Capital Gains on Equity Shares of a Company or Units of Equity-oriented Funds

As a result of Section 111A the tax on income arising to all categories of tax payers on transfer of a short-term capital asset being an equity share in a company or unit of an equity-oriented mutual fund would be only 15% (from the A.Y. 2009-2010).

However, this provision would not be applicable to all transactions of shares and units of equity mutual fund resulting in short-term capital gains but is limited only to:
transactions entered on or after 1st October 2004, and
that such transaction is chargeable to STT.

Only when both these conditions are fulfilled is the special 15% tax on such short-term capital gains applicable. It is, therefore, clear that when a short-term capital gain arises on selling equity shares or units of equity fund which does not attract STT, then the concessional rate of income tax of just 15% on short-term capital gains would not be applicable and tax would be payable on the short-term capital gains, like any other income as per applicable slab rates.

It is further provided that in the case of an individual or a Hindu undivided family, being a resident, where the total income as reduced by such short-term capital gains is below the exemption limit, then, such short-term capital gains shall be reduced by the amount by which the total income, as so reduced, falls short of the maximum amount which is not chargeable to income-tax and the tax on the balance of such short-term capital gains shall be computed at the rate of 15%. A person having short-term capital gains and other incomes, the deduction under Chapter VIA as well as the tax rebate would be allowed after reducing the said short-term capital gains.

24 No Capital Gain on Conversion of a Company to Limited Liability Partnership

As per the Finance Act, 2010 if a private limited company or a non-listed public limited company is converted into a Limited Liability Partnership (LLP), then there will be no liability to capital gains provided that certain conditions mentioned in Section 47 of the Income-tax Act, 1961 are complied with.

CHAPTER 9

Income from Interest and other investments

(SECTIONS 56 TO 59 OF I.T. ACT)

1. Introduction

Interest income whether from bank, post office, government or private companies, is liable to be assessed to income-tax. The interest income together with other incomes like income from various postal schemes, income from lottery, etc. as also other miscellaneous income which do not find place in other heads of income discussed in the preceding chapters is assessed as "Income from other sources. The dividend income as also the income from mutual funds is treated as "Income from other sources". However, on and from the A.Y. 2004-05 the entire dividend income as also the incomes from various mutual funds is exempted from tax..

2. Deductions — Section 57

The income chargeable under this head shall be computed after making the following deductions, namely:

(i) In the case of dividends, any reasonable sum paid by way of commission or remuneration to a banker or any other person for the purpose of realising such dividend on behalf of the assessee (excluding a foreign company).

(ia) Deduction as per Section 36(1) (va) [Chapter 7, para IV] in respect of income of the nature of referred to in Section 2(24)(x).

(ii) In the case of income by way of letting of plant and machinery, etc. deductions, so far as may be in accordance with the provisions of Section 30, 31, 32 and 38.

(iia) In the case of family pension standard deduction of 33-1/3% of the pension subject to maximum of ₹15,000.

(iii) Any other expenditure (not being in the nature of capital expenditure) laid out or expended wholly, and exclusively for the purpose of making or earning such income.

3. Other Provisions

Personal expenses of the assessee are not deductible from the income under this head. Likewise, the provisions of Section 40A, 40(a) (iia) and 44D are also applicable to "income from other sources" — Section 58. Similarly, the provisions of Section 41(1) are applicable for charging to tax any excessive allowance made in the past — Section 59. No deduction is allowed in computing the income from lotteries, crossword puzzles, races, card games, betting and gambling.

4. Dividends

W.e.f. the A.Y. 2004-05 dividend income would be fully tax-free in the hands of the recipient as per Section 10(34).

5. Winnings from Lotteries, Crossword Puzzles, Races, Gambling, etc. [Section 56(2)(ib)]

Income referred to in Section 2(24) (ix) shall be chargeable to tax under the head "income from other sources". Section 2(24) (ix) provides that any winnings from lotteries, crossword puzzles, races, including horse races, card games and other games of any sort including TV games or from gambling or betting or any form or nature whatsoever will be included in the definition of income. These incomes would be subject to income-tax @ 30% as per Section 115 BB.

6. Income from Units of Mutual Funds.

W.e.f. the A.Y. 2004-05 the income from units of UTI and other mutual funds [excluding capital gains] would be fully exempt from Income-tax in the hands of the recipient as per Section 10(35) of the Income Tax Act, 1961.

7. Gifts

Gifts from non-relatives in excess of ₹50,000 in a year are added as income as per Section 65(2) (vii) of the I.T. Act, 1961. This amount includes any sum of money as also immovable property and any other property. Property for this section mainly would be immovable property, shares, securities, jewellery, drawings, paintings, bullion, etc.

CHAPTER 10

Aggregation of Income and Set-off and Carry Forward of Losses

1. Introduction

Having studied the method of computing income under different heads of income as per the discussion in chapters 5 to 9, we are ordinarily in a position to compute the total income. But while computing the total income we sometimes come across certain matters not described earlier, e.g. losses incurred by the assessee in the past, or the income from certain settlements or certain credits in the books of account of the assessee which he is not able to explain satisfactorily. The problem then arises of making adjustments for such items while computing total income. It is, therefore, essential to understand certain miscellaneous provisions which directly or indirectly affect the computation of total income. Such provisions are divided into three sections in this chapter:

A. Income of other persons included in an assessee's total income.
B. Cash credits and unexplained investments, unexplained expenditure, etc.
C. Set-off or carry forward and set-off of losses.

A. Income of Other Persons Included in Assessee's Total Income — Sections 60 to 65

2. Transfers and Settlements — Sections 60 to 63

In connection with the computation of total income, the effects of transfers and settlements are as follows:

(i) All income arising to any person by virtue of transfer, whether revocable or not and effected at the time, shall be chargeable to tax as the income of the transferor (and not that of the transferee) and shall be included in his total income, if there is no transfer of the assets from which the income arises.

(ii) All income arising to any person by virtue of a revocable transfer of assets shall be chargeable to tax as the income of the transferor (and not of the transferee) and shall be included in his total income. A transfer shall be deemed to be revocable if:

(a) it contains any provision for the re-transfer directly or indirectly of the whole or any part of the income or assets to the transferor, or
(b) it, in any way, gives the transferor a right to re-assume power directly or indirectly over whole or any part of the income or assets.

Exceptions

The provision contained in (ii) above shall not apply to any income arising to any person by virtue of a transfer:

(a) by way of trust which is not revocable during the life-time of the beneficiary, and, in the cases of any other transfer, which is not revocable during the life-time of the transferee; or
(b) made before 1 April 1961, which is not revocable for a period exceeding six years.

Note: The word "transfer" as stated above includes any settlement, trust, covenant, agreement or arrangement by virtue of Secction 63(b) of the Act.

3. Income of Spouse and Daughter-in-law — Section 64(1)

In computing the total income of any individual, the income of his wife or her husband, as the case may be, and of the daughter-in law is also included in certain circumstances. The main items of income which are to be clubbed in the income of another under Section 64(1) relate to:

(1) salary, commission, fees or other remuneration to the spouse of the individual from a concern in which the latter has a substantial interest, except where the income of the spouse is only due to technical or professional qualifications and experience;
(2) gifts to the spouse of an individual;
(3) gifts to the daughter-in-law of an individual; and
(4) gifts to any trust, AOP, etc. for the benefit of the spouse or the daughter-in-law.

The husband or wife, whoever has the higher income, will be the person in whose hands the income of gift to spouse would be clubbed.

4. Clubbing of Minor's Income in Parent's Hands — Section 64(1A)

Under the provisions of Section 64(1A), effective from AY 1993-94, the income of a minor child would be clubbed with the income of the father or mother, whose income is higher. An exemption in this regard is provided under Section 10 (32) upto ₹1,500 per child.

However, from AY 1995-96 this clubbing provision is not operative where the income of the minor child is from any manual work done by him or any activity involving application of his skill, talent or specialised knowledge and experience or where the minor is a disabled person suffering from a disability of the nature described under Section 80U (Section 11).

5. Taxability of Income from Conversion of Self-acquired Property into HUF Property — Section 64(2)

Where an individual converts, at any time after 31 December 1969 his separate property into property belonging to the Hindu undivided family of which he is a member by impressing such property with the character of property belonging to the family or throwing such property into the family hotchpotch, the individual will be deemed to have transferred the converted property to the members of the family for being held by them jointly. The income from the converted property will be deemed to arise to the individual and not to the family.

B. Cash Credit, Unexplained Investments, Unexplained Expenditure, etc.

The unexplained cash credits, unexplained investments as also the unexplained expenditure are all treated as the income of the assessee and charged to tax. Similarly, Hundi loans taken by cash will be taxed as income.

C. Set-off or Carry Forward and Set-off of Losses

A loss suffered by an assessee under one source of income can be set off against another source of income under the same head of income in the same year. Similarly, the loss suffered under any head of income can be set off against income arising under any head of income other than loss under the head capital gain. The loss by way of interest on loan for residential house property can be set off against any head of income in the same year. Speculation business loss is to be set off only against speculation income. Short term capital asset loss can be set off only against capital gain, either long-term or short-term. However, the long-term capital loss can be set off only against long-term capital gain as per Section 70(3). The business loss or speculation loss or capital asset loss which cannot be set off against such incomes of the year will be carried forward for set off against the incomes of respective heads for subsequent eight years. The loss of specified type of business would be allowed to be carried forward for adjustment only with the income of the specified business.

6. No Set off of Business Loss against Salary — Section 71(2A)

An assessee shall not be entitled to set off any loss under the head "profits and gains of business or profession" against income under the head "salaries". This amendment is operative from the A.Y. 2005-06, as per the Finance (No. 2) Act, 2004.

CHAPTER 11

Deductions in Computing Total Income

[SECTIONS 80A TO 80U OF I.T. ACT]

1. Introduction

The total income as computed under different heads of income and after set-off of losses, etc. has to be further reduced by certain deductions as per Chapter VIA in the it Act, which have been amended from time to time. The deductions for the A. Y. 2011-2012 and A. Y. 2012-2013 are described below.

2. Chapter VIA in the IT Act

Chapter VIA of the IT Act provides for a straight deduction of the whole or a specified percentage of the amount qualifying for the same in computing the total income. It has been made clear in Section 80A(2) that the aggregate of these deductions cannot exceed the gross total income of the assessee.

3. Main Deductions for the A.Y. 2011-12 and the A.Y. 2012-13

I. For the A.Y. 2011-2012

(a) Deduction under Section 80C

From the A.Y. 2006-07, Individuals and HUFs are entitled to claim tax deduction under Section 80C of the Income-tax Act, 1961 by making investments in certain assets and certain stipulated expenditure upto a maximum of ₹1 lakh. This deduction is available irrespective of the taxable income of the tax payer.

The tax payers should remember that from the Financial Year 2005-06 the concept of granting tax rebate for investments, etc. made under Section 88 of the Income-tax Act 1961 has been done away with. Now as a result of insertion of new Section 80C to the Income-tax Act 1961 a deduction would be permissible to all individuals and Hindu-undivided families in respect of investment made by them, or expenses incurred by them, as mentioned in the said Section 80C of the Income-tax Act, 1961. The maximum amount that can be invested/spent for claiming the tax deduction is ₹1,00,000. The best part of the new provision is that the tax payer can invest the entire sum of of ₹1 lakh without worrying about any sub-limits used to be the case earlier. Thus, if an individual, say is interested to make payment of ₹1 lakh only for Life Insurance Premium then he can do so and enjoy full deduction to the extent of ₹1 lakh. Similarly if a person wishes no other investment to avail tax deduction then he can do and avail deduction on housing loan repayment to the full extent of ₹1 lakh. Similarly, one another person, say is interested to spend the entire ₹1 lakh on the education of his children, he can also do so and enjoy full tax benefit of deduction under the new Section 80C of the Income-tax Act, 1961.

The following is the list of main items which are eligible for aggregate tax deduction of ₹1,00,000 as per Section 80C:—

1. Payment for Life Insurance Premium.
2. Payment for Deferred Annuity Plan.
3. Deferred Annuity payable by Government.
4. Contribution to Public Provident Fund.
5. Contribution to Provident Fund set up by Central Government.
6. Contribution to Recognised Provident Fund.
7. Contribution to recognized superannuation fund.
8. Subscription to any security or deposit notified by Government.
9. Subscription to Saving Certificates.
10. Subscription for Unit Linked Insurance Plan 1971.
11. Contribution for Unit Linked Insurance Plan of LIC Mutual Fund.
12. Payment for annuity plan of LIC or any other insurer.
13. Subscription to units of notified mutual funds.
14. Contribution to notified pension fund of mutual fund.
15. Pension fund set up by National Housing Bank.
16. Subscription to a deposit scheme of. public sector company engaged in providing long term finance for housing.
17. Tuition fees of two children in India.
18. Payment of instalment for self-financing of a residential property for repayment of loan.
19. Subscription to equity shares or debentures as approved for infrastructure.

20. Subscription to any units of mutual fund as approved by the Central Board of Direct Taxes.
21. As per the Finance Act, 2006 for F.Y. 2006-07, a term-deposit for a fixed period of not less than five years with a scheduled bank would also qualify for tax deduction under Section 80C within the overall limit of ₹1 lakh. This is subject to some Rules.
22. Notified bonds of NABARD.
23. Deposit in an account under the Senior Citizens Savings Scheme Rules, 2004.
24. Five-year time deposit in an account under the Post Office Time Deposit Rules, 1981.

Note: Total amount allowed as deduction is limited to ₹1 lakh inclusive of deduction as per Section 80C, 80CCC, 80CCD and new Section 80CCE.

(b) Deduction in Respect of Contributions to Certain Pension Funds: Section 80 CCC

A deduction upto ₹10,000 used to be allowed to an individual in respect of any contribution made towards a new personal-cum-family pension scheme of lic. The amount of pension received in the hands of the contributor or the nominee shall, however, be taxable but the commuted amount received on maturity of the scheme would be totally exempt from income tax. As per the Finance Act, 2006 the maximum contribution to a pension plan can be upto ₹1 lakh but the deduction under Section 80C and Section 80CCC would be limited to maximum ₹1 lakh.

(c) Deduction in respect of Contributions to Pension Scheme of Central Government — Section 80CCD

For new entrants to Central Government service it is mandatory to contribute 10% of their salary every month to their pension account and a matching contribution is to be made by the Government. As per this section deduction is to be allowed on the whole of the amount paid or deposited as does not exceed 10% of the salary. The amount received on closure of the account or on withdrawal of the pension would be taxable. This applies to other employees as well as other individual taxpayers.

(d) Deduction for investment in Long-term Infrastructure Fund — Section 80CCF

Deduction would be available to individuals and Hindu Undivided Families on investment in approved long-term infrastructure fund. Maximum investment eligible to deduction is ₹20,000.

(e) Deduction in Respect of Medical Insurance Premia — Section 80D

A deduction upto ₹15,000 in respect of medical insurance premia for the health of the assessee or his spouse or dependent parents or dependent children or any member of the HUF would be allowed as a deduction. If such persons are senior citizens, the deduction is upto ₹20,000.

An additional deduction upto ₹15,000 to an individual would be allowed on any payment made for health insurance premia on the life of his parent or parents (whether dependent or not). If the parent is a senior citizen, the deduction would be allowed upto ₹20,000 from the A.Y. 2009-10.

(f) Deduction in Respect of Maintenance including Medical Treatment of Handicapped Dependent — Section 80DD

A resident individual or huf would be allowed a deduction upto ₹50,000 per annum in respect of any expenditure incurred on the medical treatment, training and rehabilitation of dependent relative or member and who is suffering from a permanent physical disability (including blindness) or is subject to mental retardation and is so certified by special physician, etc. and also an amount paid or deposited under any scheme of the LIC or UTI in this regard. If a person suffers from severe disability, then the deduction would be ₹1,00,000.

(g) Deduction in Respect of Medical Treatment of Terminal Ailments, etc. — Section 80DDB

A separate deduction of ₹40,000 would be allowed in the computation of the income of an individual suffering from chronic and protracted diseases and terminal ailments, or to any individual or huf on whom such individual is dependent. The diseases in respect of which the deduction would be available have been notified in the Income Tax Rules. The tax payer is required to submit a certificate in this regard from a prescribed authority every year along with his return of income. For senior citizens, the deduction is ₹60,000. This deduction is with reference to expenditure actually incurred for any amount.

(h) Deduction in Respect of Interest on Loan for Higher Education — Section 80E

Any interest on education loan will be allowed in a year for a maximum period of 8 years without any upper limit. However, no deduction would be allowed for repayment of the principal amount. The loan should be taken from a financial institution or an approved charitable organisation. This benefit will be available for any type of education after Senior Secondary Examination to an individual for self or spouse or children of the individual or the student for whom the individual is the legal guardian.

(i) Deduction in Respect of Donations to Certain Funds, Charitable Institutions, etc. — Section 80G

It provides for a straight deduction of 50% of the qualifying amount of donations (up to a maximum of 10% gross total income) in computing the total income of an assessee. For some government funds etc., it is 100%.

(j) Deduction in Respect of House Rent — Section 80GG

A deduction is allowed to an assessee not being one who has any income chargeable under the head "Salaries" and who is in receipt of any income by way of house rent allowance, in respect of house rent paid by him in excess of 10% of his total income but subject to a ceiling of 25% thereof, or ₹2,000 per month, whichever is less subject to certain other conditions like furnishing of a Form No. 10BA by the employee to the employer.

(k) Phasing out of Deductions in respect of Foreign Exchange Earnings — Sections 80HHB, 80HHBA, 80HHC, 80HHD, 80HHE, 80HHF, 80-O, 80R, 80RR & 80RRA

The deduction allowed under the various sections, as mentioned above has been phased out. Hence no deduction is available from the A.Y. 2005-06.

(l) Deduction in Respect of Bank Interest, Interest on Securities, etc. — Section 80L

On and from the A.Y. 2006-07 this deduction has been scrapped.

(m) Deduction in the Case of Permanent Physical Disability (Including Blindness) — Section 80U.

A totally blind or physically handicapped or mentally retarded individual is allowed a deduction equal to ₹50,000 in the computation of total income subject to fulfilling certain conditions. For persons with severe disability the deduction would be ₹1,00,000 from the A.Y. 2010-11.

(n) Other Deductions

There are various other deductions available to a tax payer like deduction in respect of profits and gains from industrial undertakings engaged in infrastructure development and new industrial undertakings (Section 80IA, Section 80IB and Section 80IC). Taking advantage of these deductions substantial tax deductions can be claimed by an assessee.

Under the provisions of Section 80IB(9) as amended by Finance Act, 2008 income of a refinery for mineral oil starting operations by 31.3.2012 will also get the 7-year tax holiday.

As per Section 80IB(10) certain residential housing projects are entitled to tax holiday.

The ten-year tax holiday benefit was extended to include a navigational channel in the sea as laying and operating, cross-country gas distribution network, including gas pipeline and storage facilities being an integral part of the network.

(o) Tax Holiday for Hotel and Convention Centres in NCT of Delhi and Other Areas — Section 80ID

100% deduction of the profits and gains derived from the business of convention centres and 2-star, 3-star and 4-star category hotels in NCT in Delhi and districts of Faridabad, Gurgaon, Gautam Budh Nagar and Ghaziabad, constructed and functioning between 1 April 2007 and 31 July, 2010 for a five-year period beginning from the initial assessment year would be allowed.

(p) Tax Holidays for Undertakings in North Eastern States

As per Section 80IE a deduction @ 100% for ten years would be available to certain undertakings as well as certain eligible businesses set in North Eastern States of India during the period 1.4.2007 to 31.3.2017.

(q) Five-year Holiday to Hospitals at Certain Locations - Sec. 80-1B (11C)

The Finance Act, 2008 has, w.e.f. the A.Y. 2009-10, made an amendment in Section 80-1B by inserting a new clause (11C) therein. The tax benefit of 5-year tax holiday would be extended to hospitals located anywhere in India otherwise than the excluded area, if the hospital is constructed and starts functioning between 1.4.2008 and 31.3.2013. It will be for five consecutive assessment years beginning from the initial assessment year. The excluded area would mean an area comprising the urban agglomeration of Greater Mumbai, Delhi,

Kolkata, Chennai, Hyderabad, Bangalore and Ahmedabad, the districts of Faridabad, Gurgaon, Ghaziabad, Gautam BudhNagar and Gandhinagar and the city of Secunderabad.

(r) Five-year Tax Holiday for Hotels in Districts having a World Heritage Site – Sec. 80-1D

An important amendment has been made by the Finance Act, 2008 w.e.f. the A.Y. 2009-10. The benefit of five-year tax holiday would be extended also to new two-star, three-star or four-star category hotels located in specified districts having a World Heritage Site. Such hotels are required to be constructed and start functioning at any time between 1.4.2008 and 31.3.2013. Specified districts having a World Heritage Site are districts of Agra, Jalgaon, Aurangabad, Kanchipuram, Puri, Bharatpur, Chhatarpur, Thanjavur, Bellary, South 24 Pargans (excluding Kolkata Urban Area), Chamoli, Raisen, Gaya, Bhopal, Panchmahal, Kamrup, Goalpara, Nagaon, North Goa, South Goa, Darjeeling and Nilgiri.

PART III

ASSESSMENT OF DIFFERENT ASSESSEES

CHAPTER 12

Assessment of Individuals

The following points should carefully be borne in mind:

(1) The class of an individual on the basis of his residence during a particular previous year should be ascertained. This is necessary because the incidence of tax depends upon the residence of the assessee.

(2) Whether an assessee is a member of an HUF or a partnership firm or an association of persons or a company or a combination of some or all of them should be ascertained.

(3) It should be seen whether any income from settlements or income of spouse and/or minor child, etc. is to be included in the assessee's total income as per Chapter 10.

(4) The assessee's total income should be computed (after making the deductions as per Chapter 11) to the nearest multiple of ₹10.

PROBLEM No. 10

The following are the particulars of income of an individual for the year ended 31st March, 2012:

(a) His salary is ₹7,500 p.m. and his T.A. bill for the year amounted to ₹9,000; the actual expenditure incurred by him in travelling being ₹3,000.

(b) He contributed 10% to a Provident Fund governed by the Provident Fund Act of 1925, his employer also contributing 10%. Interest on his Provident Fund account for the year amounted to ₹4,000.

Contd . . .

(c) He owns two houses, one of which is let out at ₹200 p.m. and the other (whose annual value is ₹1,000) cannot actually be occupied by him by reason of the fact that owing to his employment at Nagpur he has to reside at Nagpur itself and the residential home is not actually let and no other benefit therefrom is derived by him. The two houses are subject to local taxes of ₹150 and ₹60 per year respectively.

(d) He received ₹56,000 interest from Government securities and ₹14,000 interest on loans in the name of his minor son.

He is insured and pays an annual premium of ₹50,000 on his life policy of ₹6,00,000.

Ascertain his total income for the assessment year 2012-2013.

SOLUTION

Computation of total income for the assessment year 2012-2013:

	Rs.	Rs.
1. (a) Salary for 12 months @ ₹17,500 p.m.	2,10,000	
(b) Excess T.A. (9,000 — 3,000)	6,000	
		2,16,000
2. Income from house property:		
Rent of house let	2,400	
Less: Full local taxes	150	
Annual value of house let	2,250	
Less: Standard Deduction of 30% U/s 24	675	
		1,575
The other house is fully exempt under Section 23	—	—
3. Income from other sources:		
Interest on Government Securities	56,000	
4. Interest on loans under Section 64(1A)	14,000	70,000
Gross Total Income		2,87,575
Less: Deduction under Section 80C [21,000 + 50,000]		71,000
Total Income		2,16,575

CHAPTER 13

Assessment of Hindu Undivided Families

1. Introduction

A Hindu undivided family under the Income Tax Act is treated as a separate entity and is treated through its *karta* or manager. The concept of a joint Hindu family under this Act is different from that of a co-parcenary under the Hindu Law. Under the Income Tax Act, an HUF. is assessable in respect of the income of the common property of the family or any income having a nucleus with the joint family property, and not in respect of the member's individual earning even though they live jointly under the common mess.

2. Exemption Limit

The exemption limit for an HUF is ₹1,60,000 for the A.Y. 2010-2011 and the A.Y. 2011-2012 and ₹1,80,000 for the A.Y. 2012-2013 and ₹2,00,000 for the A.Y. 2013-2014.

3. Assessment after Partition — Section 171

Upto the period of no finding of partition recorded by an Assessing Officer, the HUF continues to be assessed as HUF. The partition of HUF can be either partial or full, but under the Income-tax Law partial partition is not recognised. After partition the individual members of the HUF are assessed in their respective hands from the income generated by partitioned assets.

PROBLEM No. 11

M/s. PQR a business house managed by an HUF consisting of three major members entitled to claim partition earned as income of ₹69,000 for the previous year ended 31.3.2012. During the course of assessment proceedings it was claimed on behalf of the members of the family that they had fully partitioned the family assets in equal shares on 1.12.2012. The profits of family upon the date of partition amounted to ₹2,60,000. The profits from the business later on carried under a firm consisting of the same members with equal shares amounted to ₹9,000 which was received as working partner's salary by each of the partners.

Contd . . .

The members claimed that the partition with effect from 1.12.2012 be accepted and the new firm be assessed as firm. The AO made necessary enquiries and accepted the fact of partition & formation of firm and the income earned by the family and passed necessary orders to that effect.

Compute the total income of the HUF and the firm and indicate the liability of the three members of the family and the firm.

SOLUTION

Upto 30.11.2012 the assessment shall be made on the HUF of PQR on ₹2,60,000. The members of the HUF are jointly and severally responsible for payment of taxes on this sum.

From 1.12.2012 the new firm has come into existence. The AO has accepted it as a firm. The firm itself is not liable to pay any tax on its income as the same is Nil, because ₹9,000 income of the firm is to be reduced by working partner's salary of ₹9,000 under Section 40 (b). Each partner i.e. P,Q and R is liable to tax on ₹3,000 in his individual assessment on salary as "Business Income" under Section 28.

4. Taxation of Income from Property Thrown into the HUF Hotchpotch by the Individual Coparcener — Section 64(2).

See para 5 of Chapter 10.

CHAPTER 14

Assessment of Firms

1. Introduction

The share of partners from the income of the firm is not to be included in computing his total income. Any salary, bonus, commission or remuneration to partners is allowed deduction as mentioned below. The income of the firm is taxed at a flat rate of 30% for the A.Y. 2012-2013 as well as for the A.Y. 2013-2014. However, income-tax would be increased by an Education Cess of 2% on I.T. and 1% Secondary and Higher Education Cess on I.T. for the A.Y. 2012-2013 and A.Y. 2013-2014. The firm (including a limited liability partnership firm) will be assessable as a firm if it has a partnership deed specifying the individual shares of the partners. A certified copy of the partnership deed signed by all partners has to be filed along with the return of income in respect of which the assessment as a firm is first sought.

2. Interest, Salary, etc. to a Partner — [Section 40(b)]

Any payment of net interest, salary, commission or remuneration made by the firm to any partner of the firm in excess of the prescribed percentage is disallowed. However, rent paid to a partner is allowable.

As a partnership firm would be assessable as such, deduction upto certain limit in respect of remuneration to working partners and interest to any partner would be allowed if so authorised by the partnership deed, upto the following limits as per Section 40(b) of the IT Act from the A.Y. 2010-11:-

For All Firms

		Rate of deduction
(a)	upto ₹3,00,000 of the book profit or in case of a loss	₹1,50,000 or at the rate of 90% of the book profit, whichever is more;
(b(	on the balance of the book profit	@ 60%

The maximum rate of interest eligible for deduction is 12% per annum simple interest. Definition of "Book Profit" and Working Partners" have been given in the Section 40(b).

CHAPTER 15

Assessment of Companies

1. Introduction

There are several special features as regards assessment of a company. Unlike most other assessees, a company is liable to pay income tax on its income, howsoever small it may be. A company pays income tax on its total income at a flat rate as fixed by the Finance Act of the year concerned. There is a uniform rate of income tax on all Indian companies which is 30% for the A.Y. 2011-2012, 2012-2013 and 2013-2014. There is surcharge @ 5% of income tax on income exceeding ₹1 crore. This would be increased by an Education Cess @ 2% on I.T. & S.C. and 1% Secondary and Higher Education Cess on I.T. & S.C. The income tax paid by a company is for the privilege which it enjoys in the shape of limited company and corporate finance and is, therefore, known as "Corporation-tax" in the Union Budget. The I.T. return for the A.Y. 2009-10 has to be filed by 30.9.2009 in Form No. 6 or 7. For later years it has to be filed by the 30th September of the succeeding year.

2. MAT on Companies — Section 115-JB

The Finance Act, 2000, from the A.Y. 2001-2002, inserted Section 115-JB in place of earlier section 115-JA, to provide for a new minimum alternate tax on companies (MAT). This provision provides that all companies having book profits under the Companies Act, prepared in accordance with Part-II and Part-III of Schedule VI to the Companies Act, would be liable to pay a minimum alternate tax at a lower rate of 7.5% (increased later). These provisions would be applicable to all corporate entitles without any exception. However, export profits under Sections 80HHC, 80HHE, and 80HHF have been kept out of purview of the provisions during the period of phasing out of the deductions available under those provisions. Likewise, the export oriented units and the units in free trade zones and eligible for exemption under Sections 10A and 10B would also be out of the purview of the provisions of the MAT. However, no credit of MAT paid under the new provisions would be available, but the credit for the brought forward MAT paid under the existing provisions would be allowed payable under the new provisions. This MAT would be applicable to all companies. As per the Finance Act, 2005 MAT will be allowed credit against future tax. subject to certain conditions. As per the Finance Act, 2006 the amount of MAT has been increased to 10% for the A.Y. 2007-2008 with inclusion of long-term capital gains otherwise exempt under Section 10(38). The Finance (No. 2) Act, 2009 has, w.e.f. the A.Y. 2010-11 increased it further to 15 %. The Finance Act, 2010 from the A.Y. 2011-2012 has increased MAT payment to 18%. Likewise, depreciation on revaluation of assets would not be admissible. As per the Finance Act, 2007 from the A.Y. 2008-2009 MAT would be levied on the book profits from enterprises exempt under Section 10A and 10B.

3. Tax on Distribution of Profits in respect of Income of Units, Mutual Funds & Dividends

The Finance Act, 2003 with effect from the A.Y. 2004-05 has amended Sections 115-0 and 115-R to provide that additional income tax at the rate of twelve and a half per cent shall be payable on distribution of income by units, mutual funds and on distribution of dividend by the companies on or after 1.4.2003. The Mutual Fund will pay tax @ 20% on the dividend distributed to all unit holders other than individuals and HUFs from 9-7-2004. The Finance Act, 2007 has, from the A.Y. 2007-2008, increased the rate of dividend distribution tax for a domestic company from 12½% to 15%. Where income is distributed by a money market mutual fund or a liquid fund, it shall pay tax on such distribution @ 25%.

CHAPTER 16

Assessment of Non-residents

1. Introduction

A "Non-resident" means a person who is not a "resident" (within the meaning of Section 6) and for the purpose of Sections 92, 93, 113 and 168, includes a person who is not ordinarily resident within the meaning of Section 6(6). The Finance Act, 2003 has amended section 6(6) of the Income Tax Act, 1961, hence the new definition must always be kept in mind to determine tax liability of Non-Resident.

The total income of any previous year of a person who is non-resident includes all income from whatever source derived which

(a) is received or is deemed to be received in India in such year by or on behalf of such person; or
(b) accrues or is deemed to accrue or arise to him in India during such year.

Thus, it is clear that non-residents are chargeable on their Indian income only.

2. Special Provisions Relating to Certain Income of Non-residents — Chapter XII-A and Section 115C to 115-I

With a view to encouraging the flow of foreign exchange remittances into India and investments in India by non-resident Indian citizens and foreign nationals of Indian origin, the IT Act has made special provisions relating to certain incomes of such non-residents.

In the case of non-resident Indians (that is to say individuals, being citizens of India or persons of Indian origin, who are not resident in India), income derived from any "foreign exchange asset'' will be charged to tax at the flat rate of 20 per cent. For the purposes of these provisions, "foreign exchange asset" means any "specified asset" acquired, purchased or subscribed to by the non-resident Indian in foreign currency in accordance with the Foreign Exchange Regulation Act, 1973 and any rules made thereunder. The "specified assets" are :

(i) Shares in an Indian company;
(ii) Debentures issued by a public limited Indian company;
(iii) Deposits with a public limited Indian company;
(iv) Securities of the central government; and
(v) Any other asset which the central government may by notification in the official gazette specify in this behalf.

In computing the income of a non-resident Indian from any foreign exchange asset, no deduction will be allowed in respect of any expenditure or allowance under any provision of the Income Tax Act.

From the A.Y. 1998-99, the provision relating to the levy of income tax at the flat rate of 10% is applied in the case of a non-resident Indian on income by way of capital gains arising on the transfer of a foreign exchange asset held by the non-resident Indian for at least 36 months (12 months in case of shares or units, etc.). However, if the net proceeds released on transfer of any foreign exchange asset are reinvested or deposited by the non-resident Indian within six months in any other specified asset or in a Non-Resident (External) Account in any bank in India or in any savings certificates notified by the central government for the purposes of Clause (4B) of Section 10 of the IT Act, the capital gains will be exempted from tax if the cost of the new asset or the amount deposited in the Non-resident (External) Account, etc. is not less than the net proceeds realised on the transfer of the foreign exchange asset. In cases where the cost of new asset, etc. is less than the net proceeds realised on transfer of the foreign exchange asset, the exemption from tax in respect of capital gains will be allowed in the same proportion as the cost of acquisition of the new asset or the amount of deposit bears to the net proceeds. In cases where the new asset, including any deposit, is transferred or converted (otherwise than by transfer) into money by the non-resident Indian within three years from the date of its acquisition, the capital gains arising from the transfer of the original foreign exchange asset, exempted from tax on the basis of the acquisition of the new asset, will be deemed to be long-term capital gain chargeable to tax in the year in which the transfer, or conversion (otherwise than by transfer) into money, of the new asset takes place.

The exemption limit for a non-resident like a resident individual is ₹1,60,000 for the Assessment Year 2011-2012, ₹1,80,000 for the Assessment Year 2012-2013 and ₹2,00,000 for the A.Y. 2013-2014.

CHAPTER 17

Assessment in Other Special Cases

[SECTIONS 159 TO 180A OF I.T. ACT]

1. Assessment of a Legal Representative, Executor, etc.

When a person dies, his legal representative shall be liable to pay any sum which the deceased would have been liable to pay if he had not died, in the like manner and to the same extent as the deceased. The legal representative of the deceased shall, for the purposes of the Act, be deemed to be an assessee under Section 159.

2. Taxation of Discretionary and Other Private Trusts — Section 164

A discretionary trust will normally be liable to tax at the maximum marginal rate of income tax. As a result, the entire income of a discretionary trust will be liable to tax at the maximum marginal rate of income tax, i.e. @ 30% plus 2% education cess and 1% secondary and higher education cess.

The discretionary trust would not be liable to tax at the maximum marginal rate in certain cases, e.g. a trust declared by Will.

3. Charge of Tax where Shares of Members in AOP. or BOI are Unknown — Section 167B

Where the individual shares of the members of an association of persons or body of individuals (other than a company or a cooperative society or a registered society) in the whole or any part of its income are indeterminate or unknown, its total income will be liable to tax at the maximum rate, namely 30% plus 2% education cess and 1% secondary and higher education cess.

4. Other Special Cases

There are various special provisions of tax, e.g. for persons trying to alienate their assets (Section 175), concessional tax treatment on know-how consideration (Section 180A), assessment of persons leaving India (Section 174), etc. Special provisions are also existing in the Income-tax Act for facilitating demergers.

PART IV

ASSESSMENT AND APPELLATE PROCEDURE

CHAPTER 18

Procedure for Assessment

[SECTIONS 139 TO 188 OF I.T. ACT]

1. Introduction

The foregoing description of the income tax law dealing with the determination of the total income of different assessees is not an end in itself. The main thing is the assessment of an assessee and the knowledge of procedure thereof.

The term "assessment" means the determination of :

(i) the total income of an assessee; and
(ii) the amount of the tax payable by him, or the amount of refund due to him.

We have already dealt with the first matter in earlier chapters. The computation of tax is contained in Appendix I. The procedure of assessment is, however, comprised of the following stages.

2. Return of Income and Assessment Procedure — Sections 139, 140, 143 & 147

The actual assessment procedure begins with the filing of a return of total income by an assessee either of his own accord or in pursuance of a notice by the Assessing Officer. With effect from AY 1989-90, it is obligatory on persons having taxable income to file returns of income voluntarily by the stipulated dates. From the A.Y. 2001-2002 all companies have to file I.T. Return. The I.T. return can be filed by individuals in Form No. 1 or Form No. 2 or Form No. 3 or Form No. 4.

Firms, AOPs and Companies have to file I.T. return in Form No. 5,6,7 or 8 as the case may be (See Chapter 24).

Due dates for filing income tax return

Section 139(1) staggers further the dates for filing the returns of income by different assessees for the A.Y. 2012-13 are given in Table I.

Table I

(1)	Where the assessee is a Company and for a person subject to tax audit under Section 44AB	By 30th September
(2)	In any other case	By 31st July

The dates given in Table I are all mandatory. The AO will not have any power to extend the dates of filing the returns.

Section 139(4) provides that a belated return can be filed within one year from the end of the relevant assessment year. Under Section 139(5), a revised return can also be filed within one year from the end of the relevant assessment year instead of 2 years earlier.

Under Section 140A not only income tax on self-assessment but also the interest to be paid for non-payment, short payment or deferment of payment of advance tax and late filing of return must be paid along with self-assessment tax. In the case of short payment, the payment will first be adjusted towards interest, and balance, if any, will be adjusted towards self-assessment tax.

As per the Taxation Laws (Amendment) Act, 2005 charitable trusts and institution coming within the purview of Section 10(23C) would be required to file return.

As per the Finance Act, 2006 the provisions relating to filing of Income-tax Return based on economic indicators have been done away with on and from the A.Y. 2006-2007.

Also as per the Finance Act, 2006 where the assessee claims tax holiday benefit under Sections 80IA, 80IAB, 80IB, 80IC, then he would be required to file the Income-tax Return by the due date. This is applicable from the Assessment Year 2006-07.

Income Escaping Assessment

Sections 147 and 148 have been substituted by new Sections and the provisions have been simplified. Any income which has escaped assessment and which comes to the notice of the assessing office subsequently can be included in assessment.

The provisions for the time limits for re-opening the assessment from 1.6.2001 are as under:

1	2
Upto 4 years from the end of the relevant assessment year If the escaped income is below ₹1 lakh	Beyond 4 years but upto 6 years from the end of the relevant assessment year If the escaped income is Rs.1,00,000 or more.

A uniform time limit of one year from the end of the financial year in which the notice under Section 148 was served has been laid in Section 153 for completion of such assessments from 1.6.2001.

The assessment has to be completed within 21 months from the end of the relevant Assessment Year.

3. Rectification of Defects in IT Return — Section 139(9)

The return will be treated as defective unless the annexures, statements and columns in the return are fully filled in and it is accompanied by a statement showing the computation of the tax payable on the basis of the return, the proof of tax, if any, claimed to have been deducted at source and the advance tax and tax on self-assessment, if any, claimed to have been paid, copies of manufacturing accounts, trading account, profit and loss account or income and expenditure account or any other similar account and balance sheet, etc.

Where the assessing officer considers that the return of income furnished by the tax-payer is defective, he is given the discretion to intimate the defects to the tax-payer and give him an opportunity to rectify the defects within a period of 15 days from the date of intimation or within such further extended time as the Assessing Officer will treat the return as an invalid return and the other provisions of the Income Tax Act will apply as if the tax-payer had failed to furnish the return. Where, however, the tax-payer rectifies the defects after the expiry of the period of 15 days from the further extended period, but before assessment is made, the assessing officer has been empowered to condone the delay and treat the return as a valid return.

4. Production of Accounts and Audit of Accounts, etc. — Sections 142 and 44AB

Before making an assessment the Assessing Officer is empowered to make necessary enquiry for the purpose of obtaining full information in respect of the income or loss of any person. He can also ask him to produce such accounts and such documents as he may require. However, he shall not require the production of any accounts relating to a period more than three years prior to the previous year.

Section 44AB provides that a person carrying on business or profession must get the accounts audited by a chartered Accountant where the total sales, turnover or gross receipts for the accounting year exceed/exceeds the limits specified. The limits, so specified are ₹60 lakh for business and ₹15 lakh for profession. Failure to do so will entail a penalty of a sum equal to one-half per cent of the total sales, turnover or gross receipts, as the case may be, subject to a maximum of ₹1,50,000. The tax audit report must be filed in time even if the IT Return is delayed.

5. Best Judgment Assessment — Section 144

If a person fails to file an Income-tax return or fails to comply with the terms of notice issued by the Assessing Officer, then in terms of Section 144 the Assessing Officer has the power to complete a best judgment assessment or ex-parte assessment. The assessee can prefer an appeal against the exparte assessment.

6. Rectification of Mistake — Sections 154 and 155

The Assessing Officer, may rectify within six months any mistake apparent from the record, either on his own motion or on an application by the assessee, within four years from the end of the financial year in which the order sought to be amended or rectified was passed.

7. Notice of Demand — Section 156

Where any tax, interest, penalty, fine or any other sum is payable in consequence of any order passed under this Act, the AO shall serve upon the assessee a notice of demand in the prescribed Form No. 7 specifying the sum so payable. The assessee must pay the demand within 30 days or any other time mentioned in the notice.

CHAPTER 19

Penalties and Prosecutions

A. Penalties

The provisions of the IT Act regarding various types of important penalties are given below :

1. Non-compliance with Summons — Section 131 and Section 272 A(1) (c)

Where a person to whom a summons is issued either to attend to give evidence or produce books of account or other documents at certain place and time, intentionally omits to attend or produce books of account or documents at the place or time, the income tax authority may impose upon him such fine not less than ₹500 and not exceeding ₹10,000 as it thinks fit.

2. Failure to Comply with Notice, Concealment of Income, etc. — Section 271

(1) The following are the types of cases covered by Section 271:

(a) Failure to comply with a notice under Section 142(1) for production of accounts, documents, etc. or under Section 143(2) for production of accounts, documents, etc., or under Section 143(2) for production of evidence etc.; the penalty for each offence is ₹10,000.

(b)Concealment of income or furnishing of inaccurate particulars of income. The minimum penalty is 100% of the tax sought to be evaded and the maximum penalty would be 300% of the tax evaded. As per the Finance Act, 2007 from 1.6.2007 there would be a minimum of 10% penalty for not recording income found during search, as per new Section 271AAA.

3. Penalty for Failure to Keep and Maintain Books of Account, etc. — Section 271A

It provides for penalty for failure to keep and maintain books of account, etc. and also for not retaining them for the prescribed period. The penalty would be ₹25,000.

4. Failure to Get Accounts Audited — Section 271B

It provides for penalty for failure to get accounts audited in respect of any previous year or obtain a report of such audit under Section 44AB or to furnish the said report along with the return of income. The penalty would be 1/2% of the total sales, turnover or gross receipts or a sum of ₹1,50,000, whichever is less.

5. Penalty for Failure to Deduct or Collect Tax at Source — Sections 271C and 271CA

If any person fails to deduct or collect the whole or any part of tax he shall be liable to pay, by way of penalty, a sum equal to the tax which he has failed to deduct or collect.

6. Penalty for Failure to Comply with the Provisions of Section 269 SS — Section 271D

If any person takes or accepts any loan or deposit in contravention of the provisions of Section 269 SS (namely, cash loan of ₹20,000 and more) he shall be liable to pay, by way of penalty, a sum equal to the amount of loan or deposit so taken or accepted by cash.

7. Penalty for Failure to Comply with the Provisions of Section 269 T — Section 271E

If any person repays deposit referred to in Section 269T by cash exceeding ₹20,000, he shall be liable to pay, by way of penalty, a sum equal to the amount of the deposit so repaid by cash.

8. Penalty for Failure to Furnish Return of Income — Section 27IF

The Finance Act, 2001 effective from 1.6.2001 provided a penalty of ₹5,000 for not filing of return by the end of the assessment year under Section 139 (1).

9. Penalty for Failure to Answer Questions, Sign Statements, etc. — Section 272A

Section 272A provides for penalty by an assessing officer or DC or CIT (Appeals) or a CIT, etc. for failure to answer questions and sign statements. The penalty in case of refusal to sign a statement, etc. would be ₹10,000 for each such default and the maximum penalty would be Rs.10,000 for each such default. For failure to furnish return, etc. a penalty of ₹100 per day of default can be levied.

10. Penalty for Failure to Comply with Section 133B — Section 272AA

A penalty upto ₹1,000 can be levied under this provision.

11. Penalty for Failure to Comply with Section 203A — Section 272BB

A penalty of ₹10,000 can be levied for failure to comply with the provisions of Section 203A.

The Finance Act, 2001, with effect from 1.6.2001, amended various penalty provisions to remove the minimum and maximum penalties. Only one penalty is now provided under different sections as given below:

Section 271(1)(ii)	—	Rs.10,000
Section 271A	—	Rs.25,000
Section 272A	—	Rs.10,000
Section 272BB	—	Rs.10,000
Section 271F	—	₹ 5,000

Besides, there are some new penalties under Sections 271AA, 271BA and 271G.

12. Penalty for Failure to Furnish Annual Information Return –Section 285 BA & 271 FA

Even the Government agencies and other authorities would be required to furnish an annual information return regarding a financial transaction exceeding ₹50,000 which is recorded on or after 1.4.2004, to the prescribed authority. A penalty of ₹100 per day of failure would be leviable.

13. Reduction or Waiver of Penalty by the CIT — Section 273A

The Chief CIT or the CIT has the power to reduce or waive penalty under Section 271(c). For qualifying for reduction or waiver of penalty under Section 273A apart from making voluntarily and in good faith full and true disclosure of his income the assessee should also have paid the tax on the basis of his return.

14. Bar of Limitation for Imposing Penalties — Section 275

It provides that no order imposing a penalty under Sections 271 to 274 will be passed

(a) in a case where the order is subject matter of appeal to the DC(Appeals) or CIT (Appeals) under Section 246 or an appeal to the Tribunal by the AO(and not in the case of an appeal to the Tribunal by the assessee) under Section 253(2) after the expiration of a period of

- (i) two years from the end of the financial year in which the proceeding in the course of which penal action for imposition of penalty has been initiated are completed; or
- (ii) six months from the end of the month in which the order of the DC(A) or the CIT(Appeals) or, as the case may be, the Tribunal is received by the CIT whichever period expires later;

(b) in any other case, after the expiration of two years from the end of the financial year in which the proceedings, in the course of which action for imposition of penalty has been initiated, are completed.

In computing the period of limitation for the purpose of this Section certain periods are to be excluded.

As per the Taxation Laws (Amendment) Act, 2005 in the case of an assessee, the Assessment Order etc. is in appeal before the CIT (Appeals) or Income-tax Appellate Tribunal or High Court or the Supreme Court, etc. and the order imposing or enhancing or reducing or cancelling penalty or dropping the proceedings for the imposition of penalty is passed before the appellate order then the order the imposing or enhancing or reducing or cancelling penalty or dropping the proceedings for the imposition of penalty may be passed on the basis of assessment as revised by giving effect to such order of the Appellate authority, etc. The assessee would be given a reasonable opportunity of being heard. The revised order cannot be passed after the expiry of six months from the end of the month in which the order was passed by the higher authority. This has been done by introducing new Section 155 (11A).

B. Prosecutions

The minimum punishment generally is rigorous imprisonment for 3 months and where the tax involved exceeds ₹1 lakh, it is 6 months. The maximum punishment is rigorous imprisonment for three years and 7 years respectively. It is not only taxpayers but their advisers and accountants, etc. who abet in the commission of the offences who can also be punished likewise. Prosecution is launched generally where an assessee wilfully evades payment of tax or fails to pay tax or penalty, or file a return in time (in cases where the net tax payable on regular assessment exceeds ₹3,000), etc.

Punishment for offences by a company would be on concerned officer from 1.10.2004 — Section 278B. This amendment is by the Finance (No. 2) Act, 2004.

Falsification of books of account and documents is also made punishable from 1.10.2004 — New Section 277A. This amendment is by the Finance (No.2) Act, 2004.

C. Penal Interest

(a) Sections 234A, 234B and 234C have been inserted with mandatory charge of interest for certain defaults. Section 234A provides for charge cf interest for belated filing of return at 1% per month for every month or part of the month of default.

(b) Interest for default in payment of advance tax will be charged under Section 234B at the rate of 1% for every month or part of the month.

(c) Section 234C provides for charge of interest where there has been deferment of instalment of advance tax at the rate of 1% p.m. For the shortfall till 15th March the interest rate is 1% of the shortfall.

(d) New Section 234D provides for charge of interest at ½% per month on excess refund of tax on summary assessment.

(e) Section 244A specifies that interest shall be payable by Government on refund of tax or penalty at ½% per month.

(f) Penal interest for non-compliance with the TDS provisions would be 1½% per month or part of the month.

CHAPTER 20

Collection and Recovery of Tax

1. Different modes of tax payment

Under the Act, the following are the three main modes of collecting taxes:

(I) Payment by deduction of tax at source;
(II) Direct payment of tax

- (a) Advance payment of tax,
- (b) Payment as a result of self-assessment under Section 140A,
- (c) Payment as a result of regular assessment under Section 143 or Section 144,
- (d) Payment in any other special manner.

(III) Collection of Income Tax.

Payment by deduction of tax at source or by advance payment of tax are mentioned under Section 190. The levy of tax by direct payment is provided by Section 191 only when the tax is not deductible at source and where the tax has not in fact been deducted at source in accordance with the provisions of the Act.

2. Types of income subject to deduction of tax at source

The following types of incomes are mainly subject to deduction of tax at source:

- (a) Salaries — Section 192.
- (b) Interest on securities — Section 193.
- (c) Dividend — Section 194.
- (d) Other interest — Section 194A.
- (e) Winnings from Lottery or crossword puzzle — Section 194B.
- (f) Winning from horse race — Section 194BB.
- (g) Payment to resident contractors and sub-contractors — Section 194C.

(h) Insurance commission — Section 194D.

(i) Payments to non-resident sportsmen or sports associations — Section 194E.

(j) Payments in respect of deposits under the N.S.S. — Section 194EE.

(k) Payments on account of repurchase of units by Mutual Fund or UTI — Section 194F.

(l) Commission, etc., on the sale of lottery tickets — Section 194G.

(m) Commission or brokerage — Section 194H.

(n) Rent exceeding ₹1,20,000 — Section 194 I.

(o) Fees for professional or technical services — Section 194J.

(p) Income from UTI units and Mutual Funds — Section 194K

(q) Other sums payable to non-residents and non-Indian companies only — Section 195.

(r) Income from units — Section 196B.

(s) Income from foreign currency bonds or shares of Indian company — Section 196 C.

(t) Income of foreign institutional investors from Securities — Section 196D.

(u) Payment of compensation on acquisition of certain immovable property in excess of ₹1 lakh-new Section 194LA.

3. Incidental Aspects of TDS

TDS is applicable under different sections in different circumstances and at different levels of income. For example, TDS under Section 194A is applicable only where the interest payable exceeds ₹5,000. Further, individuals and HUFs cannot deduct tax at source under Section 194A. Likewise, TDS under Section 194B is applicable only on the lottery winnings exceeding ₹5,000, etc. In respect of TDS from "salary" income of an employee, the estimated salary is considered and benefit under Sections 80C, 80CCC, 80L or 88 is allowed by the employer at the time of TDS. Persons deducting tax at source are required to give certificate of TDS in Form No. 16A or 16AA, etc. to the person concerned. Income payable "net of tax" has to be grossed up as per Section 195A.

A senior citizen who is not liable to pay any tax will not be subject to TDS on filing a self-declaration in Form No. 15-H u/s 197A (1C).

Some important items of tax rates for deduction of tax at source during the F.Y. 2011-2012 are given on next page:

1. Salary	At the rates prescribed.
2. Interest	10%, 20% for companies when interest exceeds ₹5,000/- p.a. (₹10,000 for bank interest, etc.)
3. Lottery winnings, etc.	30% when payment exceeds ₹10,000.
4. Winnings on Horce race	30% when payment exceeds ₹5,000.
5. Payment to contractor & sub-contractor	@ 1% for Individuals & HUFs and 2% in other cases on contracts exceeding ₹20,000 each time or ₹50,000 in the aggregate.
6. Payments out of NSS (Old)	@ 20% when payment exceeds ₹2,500 in a year.
7. Commission	@ 10% when payment exceeds ₹5,000 p.a.
8. Rent	@ 2% for rent for plant, machinery and equipment @ 10% for rent exceeding ₹1,80, 000.
9. Professional fee and royalty	@ 10% of payment exceeding ₹30,000 per annum.
10. Compensation	@ 10% on amount in excess of ₹1,00,000.

The sellers of alcholic liquor, forest produce, scrap, timber are required to deduct tax at source when they sell such products.

Likewise tax collection at source on cash purchase of gold jewellery in excess of ₹ 5 lakh and bullion purchased in excess of ₹ 2 lakh.

4. Advance Payment of Tax — Sections 207 to 219.

The following are the salient features of the procedure regarding advance tax.

(a) Where advance tax is payable, the assessee shall himself compute the advance tax payable on his current income at the rates in force in the financial year and deposit the same whether or not he has been earlier assessed. He need not file any estimate.

(b) Under Section 211 upto 30%, 60% and 100% of the advance tax payable shall be paid by non-company assessees by 15th Sept., 15th Dec. and 15th March respectively. Any payment for advance tax before 31st March will be treated as advance tax. The threshold limit for the applicability of advance tax is ₹10,000 from the FY. 2009-2010.

The quantum of advance tax payable during the financial year 2011-12 by company taxpayers is as under:

(i) On or before 15th June	- 15%
(ii) On or before 15th September	- 45%
(iii) On or before 15th December	- 75%
(iv) On or before 15th March	-100%

(c) In case Advance tax has not been paid in time or there is deferment of Advance tax, then penal interest would be payable.

As per the Taxation Laws (Amendment) Act, 2005, the definition of rent for the purposes of TDS has been amended to provide for TDS even on hiring and leasing of equipments, etc. Non-compete fees and exclusivity rights would also be subject to TDS.

CHAPTER 21

Refunds

[SECTIONS 237 TO 245]

1. Origin of Refunds — Section 237

If any person satisfies the assessing officer that the amount of tax paid by him or on his behalf or treated as paid by him or on his behalf for any assessment year exceeds the amount with which he is properly chargeable under this Act for that year, he shall be entitled to refund of the excess. The refund of tax would be rounded off to the nearest multiple of ten rupees

2. Form of Claim for Refund and Limitation — Section 239

Every claim under these sections shall be made in the prescribed Form No. 30 obtainable from the Assessing Officer and verified in the prescribed manner. Such a claim must be made within one year from the last day of the assessment year in which the income in respect of which the claim is made was assessable.

3. Refund on Appeal, etc. — Section 240

Where, as a result of any order passed in appeal or other proceeding under this Act, refund of any amount becomes due to an assessee, the AO shall, except as otherwise provided in this Act, refund the amount to the assessee without his having to make any claim in that behalf.

4. Interest on Refunds — Section 244A

Interest at ½% per month from 1st April of the assessment year upto the date of refund will be allowed to the assessee. If the refund is less than 10% of the tax as determined on regular assessment, no interest is payable. In the case of other refund interest is calculated @ ½% per month for every month from the date of payment of tax or penalty to the date of grant of refund. Where, as a result of appellate order, the amount on which interest was payable is increased or reduced, the interest shall be increased or reduced accordingly. Thus interest payable on refund by the Central government (Income Tax Department) would be ½% per month.

CHAPTER 22

Appeals, Revisions & References

(SECTIONS 246 TO 269 OF I.T. ACT)

1. Right of appeal — Section 246 A

The right of appeal is given only to the taxpayer and not the department. Therefore, the department cannot go in appeal against any order of the AO to the CIT (Appeals). The various kinds of appeals permissible under the I.T. Act are given below.

2. First Appeal to the CIT (Appeals) — Sections 246 to 251

The first appeal lies to the CIT (Appeals). An appeal should ordinarily be filed in Form No. 35 within 30 days of the service of a notice or order against which the appeal is to be preferred. Filing fee has been fixed at a minimum of ₹250 and a maximum of ₹1,000 where the assessed total income is over ₹2 lakh. Where the appeal is not relatable to the assessed income the filing fee is ₹250.

An appeal to CIT (Appeals) against an assessment order would be barred unless the admitted portion of the tax has been paid before filing the appeal.

3. Revision by Commissioner (CIT) — Sections 263 to 264

Where the stake involved is small, an assessee can apply to the CIT within 1 year from the date of order passed by an authority subordinate to CIT The application must be accompanied with a fee of ₹500.

4. Appeals to Income Tax Appellate Tribunal (ITAT) — Sections 252 to 255

A further appeal lies to the Appellate Tribunal against the order of the AO. Where the total income as computed by the AO exceeds ₹1 lakh, but does not exceed ₹2 lakh, the fee payable by the assessee is ₹1,500.

Where the assessed income exceeds ₹2 lakhs, it shall be 1% of the assessed income, subject to a maximum of ₹10,000.

The period of limitation for appeal to the Appellate Tribunal is 60 days from the date on which the order is communicated to the assessee or commissioner.

5. Direct Appeals to High Court — Sections 260A and 260B

An appeal would lie against the orders of the Tribunal directly to the High Court (to be filed within 120 days) if the High Court is satisfied that the case involves a substantial question of law.

6. Appeal to the Supreme Court — Sections 261 to 262

An appeal shall lie to the Supreme Court from the judgment of a high court if the high court certifies that the case is a fit one for appeal to the Supreme Court.

CHAPTER 23

Calculation of Tax

(For A.Y. 2011-12 and A.Y. 2012-13)

1. Introduction

The Income Tax Act, 1961 relates to income tax only. It deals merely with the basis, the method and machinery of assessment. It does not contain a schedule of rates at which tax is to be charged. The rates of tax are determined by the Finance Act passed annually by the Parliament.

2. Rates of Income Tax for A.Y. 2011-12 and A.Y. 2012-13

Substantial changes have been made by the Finance Act, 2011, for exemption limit and the rates of tax for TDS on "Salaries", computation of "advance tax" during the F.Y. 2011-12 (relevant to the A.Y. 2012-13). Thus, the basic exemption limit is increased from ₹1,60,000 to ₹1,80,000 for all male individuals, HUFs, AOP, BOL and artificial juridical persons. The new rates of I.T. on total income in such cases would be as under (for the A.Y. 2012-13):

(i) For the A.Y. 2012-2013, the rates of income tax:

(A) For a male individual:

Upto	₹1,80,000	Nil
From	₹1,80,000 to ₹5,00,000	10%
From	₹5,00,001 to ₹8,00,000	20%
Above	₹8,00,000	30%

(B) For a Women below 60 years:

In the case of every individual, being a woman resident in India, and below the age of sixty years at any time during the previous year the rate of I.T. would be as under:

Upto	₹1,90,000	Nil
From	₹1,90,001 to ₹5,00,000	10%
From	₹5,00,001 to ₹8,00,000	20%
Above	₹8,00,000	30%

(C) For a Senior Citizen (60 years or more):

In the case of every individual, being a resident in India, who is of the age of sixty years or more at any time during the previous year:

Upto	₹2,50,000	Nil
From	₹2,50,001 to ₹5,00,000	10%
From	₹5,00,001 to ₹8,00,000	20%
Above	₹8,00,000	30%

(D) For a Senior Citizen (80 years or more):

In the case of every individual, who is of the age of 80 years or more at any time during the previous year the rate of I.T. would be as under:

Upto	₹5,00,000	Nil
From	₹5,00,001 to ₹8,00,000	20%
Above	₹8,00,000	30%

(ii) For the A.Y. 2011-2012 the rates of income tax:

(A) For a Male Individual

Upto	₹1,60,000	Nil
From	₹1,60,000 to ₹5,00,000	10%
From	₹5,00,001 to ₹8,00,000	20%
Above	₹8,00,000	30%

(B) For Resident Woman (below 65 years)

Upto	₹1,90,000	Nil
From	₹1,90,001 to ₹5,00,000	10%
From	₹5,00,001 to ₹8,00,000	20%
Above	₹8,00,000	30%

(C) For a Resident Senior Citizen (65 Years or more)

Upto	₹2,40,000	Nil
From	₹2,40,001 to ₹5,00,000	10%
From	₹5,00,001 to ₹8,00,000	20%
Above	₹8,00,000	30%

In all the above cases there will be no Surcharge. The Education Cess of 2% and the "Secondary & Higher Education Cess" of 1% would continue in all cases.

For the cooperative societies, firms, local authorities, domestic companies, the rates of I.T., S.C. & two cesses for the F.Y. 2011-2012 (relevant to A.Y. 2012-2013) would continue to be same as for the A.Y. 2011-2012.

The companies having income in excess of ₹1 crore would pay surcharge of 5% in the F.Y. 2011-2012 as against 7.5% for the A.Y. 2011-2012.

N. B.The rates of I.T. for the A.Y. 2013-2014 are different.

3. Computation of Net Agricultural Income for Purpose of Income Tax for AY 2011-2012

Agricultural income is, generally speaking, exempt from income tax. However, agricultural income (in excess of ₹5,000) has to be taken into account for determining the rate of tax applicable to non-agricultural income. This is known as partial integration of agricultural and non-agricultural income. This applies to individuals, HUFs, AOPs. and artificial juridical persons only.

For the purpose of determining the rate of income tax applicable to the non-agricultural portion of the tax-payer's income for F.Y 2011-2012, i.e. A.Y. 2012-13 the first ₹1,80,000 of this non-agricultural income will be appropriated to the lowest slab which is exempt from tax. The agricultural income will be appropriated to the middle slabs and the balance of non-agricultural income will be appropriated to the upper slab of agricultural income.

4. Computation of Assessment and Tax

The following successive steps are necessary in order to prepare the assessment of an assessee:

(1) Computation of the gross total income and total income in the manner explained in chapters 5 to 11. Adding up the various amounts of tax already deducted or otherwise paid at source, or collected at source, etc., separately. Determining the net agricultural income as per para 3.

(2) Calculation of the amount of income tax chargeable on the total income.

(3) Deduction of the amount of tax paid in advance under Section 209A or 210 or 212 and interest thereon (if any) and also tax paid under Section 206C and grant rebate of tax under Sections 88 & 88B.

(4) Deduction of the amount paid under Section 140A, i.e. under self-assessment or otherwise.

(5) The balance will then be the net amount of tax payable or refundable. Add the amount of interest, if any, and you arrive at the total amount payable or refundable.

HAPTER 24

Do it Yourself Guide to Filing Your Income Tax Return

As and when the month of July starts the news start appearing that individuals have to file their income-tax return by 31st July. Of course, the date is extended in some cases in some of the years.

It is absolutely necessary for all individuals to know as to when it is compulsory for a person to file an income-tax return. Income-tax return is required to be filed every year for the financial year known as assessment year, e.g., the present assessment year is 2012-2013. In this, the income of previous financial year also technically known as "previous year" is to be shown. Thus, the previous year for the assessment year 2012-2013 is the year from 1.4.2011 and ending on 31.3.2012 that is the financial year 2011-2012.

Thus, if any person has taxable income exceeding the exemption limit of ₹1,80,000 for all male individuals or ₹1,90,000 for women tax payers or ₹ 2,50,000 for senior citizens or ₹5,00,000 for super senior citizens of the age of 80 years or more then, he (which includes she) has to file the income-tax return on a compulsory basis. This is so even if the person happens to be a salaried-employee even if full tax is deducted at source. Likewise, even if deduction of tax at source is there in respect of other incomes, but if a professional person has taxable income exceeding ₹1,80,000, then such person has also to file the return.

If a person carries on small business and does not maintain regular books of account even then he can file the income-tax return by estimating his net business income @ 8% of the total turnover under Section 44AD. This advantage can be taken of only by persons engaged in business and having gross turnover or receipts upto ₹60 lakh. This scheme is applicable to individuals, HUFs and partnership firms excluding limited liability partnership firms. It is also not available to an assessee availing deductions under Section 10A, 10AA, 10B, 10BA or certain deductions under chapter VI A (c). As per the Finance Act 2006, the compulsory filing of income tax return based on economic criteria has been deleted from the A.Y. 2006-2007.

Which Form

When the individual knows his obligation to file the income-tax return, the next decision to be taken by him is about the type of income-tax return form to choose. Various forms are prescribed for different types.

From the A.Y. 2007-2008 new Income Tax Return Forms have been prescribed. Return Form No. 1 is for individuals having salary and interest income and no other income. Form No. 2 is for individuals and HUFs having income from any source except from business or profession while Form No. 3 is the return of income for individuals and HUFs being partners in firms and not having proprietary business or profession. The Income Tax Return Form No. 4 is for individuals and HUFs having proprietary business or profession. A partnership firm has to file I.T. return in Form No. 5 and a company in Form No. 6. A charity trust has to file the I.T. return in Form No. 7. An FBT return can be filed in Form No. 8 or in Form No. 5 or 6, as the case may be.

Last Date

Normally, the last date for voluntarily filing of income-tax return is 31st July of the assessment year concerned. This may be extended sometimes. In some cases, the income-tax return can also be filed on or before the last date of the assessment year concerned or within one year thereof, however, with penal interest. Where a person is carrying on a business having a turnover exceeding ₹10 lakh, then tax audit becomes compulsory and the last date for filing the income-tax return in such cases is 30th September from the A.Y. 2008-2009. For persons claiming income-tax refund also the income-tax return should be filed as early as possible but not later than one year from the end of the assessment year concerned. Thus, for claiming refund for the assessment year 2012-2013, the income-tax return with the refund Form No.30 can be filed any time on or before 31.3.2014.

Penalty for non filing

It may be noted that a person who is required to file a return of income compulsorily is liable to a penalty of ₹5,000 for not filing the return by the end of the assessment year concerned. It may also be noted here that there is no provision for any minimum or maximum penalty in this case. However, for failure to file the IT return in time, with a reasonable cause, penalty may not be levied.

How to fill in

The filling in of the income-tax return form appears to be a tedious affair but it is not so. Any new income-tax payer or any tax payer not conversant with the technical provisions of the Income-tax Law can approach the Public Relations Officer of the Income Tax Department for help in filling in the Income-tax Return form. The particulars of Form No. 1 or 2 are not at all very complicated. Two copies of the income-tax return form have to be filled in. One copy will be signed and returned to the tax payer and the other copy would be retained by Income tax Department. For example, the name, the father's name, the address, the telephone, date of birth, male or female, etc., can easily be given. Permanent Account Number must be given by every person. If no application has been made for the Permanent Account Number, the same should be made well in time. Where no Permanent Account Number has been allotted, then a copy of the application form should be enclosed with the return form. As regards, the details about the income computation from salary, house property, other sources, etc., the same are explained in the form itself. For example, while computing the income from the house property, as per the Form No. 2, 30% of the annual value (rental value less municipal taxes) is deductible. Besides, interest on loan taken for the acquisition of property is also deductible. There may be certain deductions in respect of payments for Insurance, PF, PPF, etc. as per Section 80C or payment for charitable donations, Mediclaim policy premium. These should be filled in properly and deducted from the gross total income to arrive at the taxable income. Tax paid as advance tax or tax deducted at source i.e., TDS should be shown in the relevant columns. The net amount at the end would represent the amount of tax payable on self assessment or refundable to the assessee.

Where the I.T. Department's receiving section does not accept the I.T. return, the same can be sent by registered post acknowledgement due.

Accompanying Papers

Though the new I.T. return form does not mention about the various papers to be enclosed along with the income-tax return, yet it is necessary for the tax payers to file copies of the proof of payment for claiming tax deduction under Section 80C like Life Insurance premium, Public Provident Fund contribution, or for deduction in respect of charitable donations, etc separately or when so demanded by the Assessing Officer. Likewise, certificates of deduction of tax at source and copies of tax challan should not be enclosed. Where there is capital gain shown in Form No. 2, then the computation sheet for capital gains and the copy of the document concerning sale of the capital assets should also be sent separately. The golden rule to remember in this case is that every paper which helps in proving the payment of tax or claim of rebate or deduction or to explain any special feature of any income must be sent separately to avoid hassles. It is always better to send all relevant papers and documents later to avoid reassessment tax proceedings at a later stage. Power is also available to the employer to file Income-tax return in the electronic return form on behalf of the employees.

CHAPTER 25

Income Tax Rates for the A.Y. 2012-2013

(Individuals and Hindu Undivided Families)

[As per the Finance Act, 2012]

For the A.Y. 2012-2013

(i) In the case of every individual or Hindu Undivided Family or association of persons or body of individuals, whether incorporated or not, or every artificial juridical person.

Rates of Income Tax

1. Where the total income does nct exceed ₹1,80,000	Nil
2. Where the total income exceeds ₹1,80,000 but does not exceed ₹5,00,000	10 per cent of the amount by which the total income exceeds ₹1,80,000.
3. Where the total income exceeds ₹5,00,000 but does not exceed ₹8,00,000	₹32,000 *plus* 20 per cent of the amount by which the total income exceeds ₹5,00,000.
4. Where the total income exceeds ₹8,00,000	₹92,000 *plus* 30 per cent of the amount by which the total income exceeds ₹8,00,000.

(ii) In the case of every individual, being a woman resident in India, and below the age of sixty years at any time during the previous year:

1. Where the total income does not exceed ₹1,90,000	Nil

2. Where the total income exceeds ₹1,90,000 but does not exceed ₹5,00,000	10 per cent of the amount by which the total income exceeds ₹1,90,000.
3. Where the total income exceeds ₹5,00,000 but does not exceed ₹8,00,000	₹31,000 *plus* 20 per cent of the amount by which the total income exceeds ₹5,00,000.
4. Where the total income exceeds ₹8,00,000	₹91,000 *plus* 30 per cent of the amount by which the total income exceeds ₹8,00,000.

(iii) In the case of every individual, being a resident in India, who is of the age of sixty years or more but less than eighty years at any time during the previous year:

1. Where the total income does not exceed ₹2,50,000	Nil
2. Where the total income exceeds ₹2,50,000 but does not exceed ₹5,00,000	10 per cent of the amount by which the total income exceeds ₹2,50,000.
3. Where the total income exceeds ₹5,00,000 but does not exceed ₹8,00,000	₹25,000 *plus* 20 per cent of the amount by which the total income exceeds ₹5,00,000.
4. Where the total income exceeds ₹8,00,000	₹85,000 *plus* 30 per cent of the amount by which the total income exceeds ₹8,00,000.

(iv) In the case of every individual, being a resident in India, who is of the age of eighty years or more at any time during the previous year:

1. Where the total income does not exceed ₹5,00,000	Nil

2.	Where the total income exceeds ₹5,00,000 but does not exceed ₹8,00,000	20 per cent of the amount by which the total income exceeds ₹5,00,000.
3.	Where the total income exceeds ₹8,00,000	₹60,000 *plus* 30 per cent of the amount by which the total income exceeds ₹8,00,000.

Note: The above tax has to be increased by 2% Education Cess plus 1% Secondary and Higher Education Cess.

CHAPTER 26

Income Tax Rates for the A.Y. 2013-2014

(Individuals and Hindu Undivided Families)

[As per the Finance Act, 2012]

For the A.Y. 2013-2014

(i) In the case of every individual or Hindu Undivided Family or association of persons or body of individuals, whether incorporated or not, or every artificial juridical person.

Rates of Income Tax

Upto ₹2,00,000 of total income	Nil
₹2,00,001 to ₹5,00,000 of total income	10 per cent
₹5,00,001 to ₹10,00,000 of total income	20 per cent
Above ₹10,00,000 of total income	30 per cent

(ii) In the case of every individual, being a resident in India, who is of the age of sixty years or more but less than eighty years at any time during the previous year:

Upto ₹2,50,000 of total income	Nil
₹2,50,001 to ₹5,00,000 of total income	10 per cent
₹5,00,001 to ₹10,00,000 of total income	20 per cent
Above ₹10,00,000 of total income	30 per cent

(iii) In the case of every individual, being a resident in India, who is of the age group of eighty years or more at any time during the previous year:

Upto ₹5,00,000 of total income	Nil
₹5,00,001 to ₹10,00,000 of total income	20 per cent
Above ₹10,00,000 of total income	30 per cent

No surcharge shall be levied in the cases of persons covered under paragraph-A of part-III of the First Schedule.

Note: The above tax has to be increased by 2 per cent Education Cess plus 1 per cent Secondary and Higher Education Cess.